Leather

Josephine Barbe

Photographs by
Frank-Michael Arndt

History
Techniques
Projects

4880 Lower Valley Road • Atglen, PA 19310

About the Author

Josephine Barbe studied fine arts, graduating with a master's degree in textile design at the Hochschule der Künste, Berlin (today, UdK), where she learned how to work leather. She specialized in her field by working at the leather boutique "Kunst am Körper" (Art on the Body) in Berlin, where she manufactured clothing, bags, belts, and hats made from leather. Today, she is a scientific fellow at the Technical University Berlin, where she lectures and holds seminars about textile manufacturing. She also offers seminars at her own workshop and participates in textile shows.

Proof reading: Heidi Müller, CH, Bern
Layout: Atelier Mühlberg, CH, Basel
Photography: Frank-Michael Arndt and Josephine Barbe
Drawings: Josephine Barbe
Translated from German by Jonee Tiedemann
Originally published as *Leder: Geschichte – Techniken – Projekte,* by Haupt Verlag, Bern, Stuttgart, Wien. Copyright © 2007 Haupt Bern.

Type set in TheSans

ISBN: 978-0-7643-4484-8
Printed in China

Published by Schiffer Publishing, Ltd.
4880 Lower Valley Road
Atglen, PA 19310
Phone: (610) 593-1777; Fax: (610) 593-2002
E-mail: Info@schifferbooks.com

For our complete selection of fine books on this and related subjects, please visit our website at www.schifferbooks.com. You may also write for a free catalog.

This book may be purchased from the publisher. Please try your bookstore first.

We are always looking for people to write books on new and related subjects. If you have an idea for a book, please contact us at proposals@schifferbooks.com

Schiffer Publishing's titles are available at special discounts for bulk purchases for sales promotions or premiums. Special editions, including personalized covers, corporate imprints, and excerpts can be created in large quantities for special needs. For more information, contact the publisher.

Contents

Introduction

Leather is supple and soft, tough, durable, and sometimes it is quite hard — part protection, part decoration. It is an ideal material for many objects which surround us daily. Leather is the classic material for bags, garments, saddles, book bindings, and furniture upholstery. Because of its properties, it is suited well for these different items.

This book shows the flexibility of this chameleon-like material and provides background information about its history, tradition and basic techniques for the working of leather. The projects which are presented — garments, bags, jewelry and interior accessories — can be manufactured with a home sewing machine and a few simple tools. The level of difficulty ranges from easy (☺) to medium (☺☺) to difficult (☺☺☺) and is indicated with each project.

If you like working with felt, you will love working with leather. Felt and leather are natural and archaic materials, both from animals. Because of this, their properties are similar: leather and felt are easy to shape and their smooth cut edges, worked without smoothing them in any way, provides unusual effects. The combination of both materials is particularly beautiful, and leather as an appliqué on felt has been used since early times to provide longevity.

Certainly this book does not cover the topic of leather completely, but it does provide a wealth of practically oriented information about this special material, together with a selection of projects which are, at the same time, *en vogue* and timeless.

I hope that you will develop many new ideas — with leather, of leather, and on leather.

—Josephine Barbe

1

Leather

And God the Lord made for Adam and his wife garments of skins and clothed them.

—**Genesis**

1.1 **Etymology**

Leather signifies "tanned animal skin." The term is derived from the Celtic form lethar, leddr, but it is uncertain whether the Germanic word "Leder" is derived from the Celtic or related to it. The adjective "leathery" implies the toughness of something. In Middle High German, the noun also indicates several different objects made from leather, for example the sword's sheath. A German expression invokes the tearing and shearing of leather to denote someone's hard attack, as well as the exuberant showing off.

Up until the 16th century the term was used to denote both animal and human skin as hide. The phrase "having a thick hide" becomes more understandable with this background. Luther's translation of the Bible begins the differentiation between the animal skin, the hide, and the skin, for humans.

What we call skin is an organ consisting of several layers, which covers the entire surface of animals and humans. In German, the word is *die haut,* derived from terms such as hat, hut, or house, signifying coverage, surrounding, protecting. If the protection fails, something gets under your skin.

The History of Leather

When man learned how to wrap pieces of leather around his feet to protect them from stones and thorns, he was able to walk faster. When he found out that water could be transported in a leather bag, he could walk further. And when he covered his body with hides, he was protected from the elements.

The history of leather is about as old as the history of human culture. There are no remaining pieces of leather from the very beginning of human history, the early Stone Age. But there have been dicoveries of stone and bone tools that were likely used for the making of clothes. Hand axe, hide scraper, flaying knife, shaver, smoother, awl and graver may have been used for the working of hides. Even the sewing needle was known in the early Stone Age.

The original human garment may have been a loincloth made from the hide of a hunted animal, as was customary among the Egyptians. The findings in graves from prehistoric times show that leather is one of the oldest materials to have been adorned with artistic designs. An Egyptian grave at Gebelien yielded what is arguably the oldest leather container, from 4000 BC. It features engraved lines in the shape of a leaf.

Leather articles in Egypt were as valuable as gold and ivory. If they were not walking barefoot, the Egyptians of the higher class were wearing sandals. The first models were very simple and consisted of a sole held on the foot with a triangular lace configuration.

Thanks to new tanning methods, the Romans succeeded in manufacturing many objects for day-to-day life with comparatively little difficulty. The leather sandal became the footwear of the common people as well. The Roman senators wore "calceus," high black or red leather shoes with lacings above the instep, and the uniform of the Roman soldiers included a leather cap.

Saint Crispin lived around 300 AD. He came from a noble Roman family and had escaped the persecutions of Diocletian. In Soissons, he learned the craft of shoe making and made shoes for the poor, for free. But he connected his service to the poor with the conversion to Christianity. As punishment, he was severely tortured and ultimately beheaded. But as a martyr, Crispin became the patron saint of the shoemakers and tanners.

Marco Polo, the Venetian world traveler, merchant, and discoverer, returned from China in the 13th century and brought back with him the news about Chinese leather-working methods. He told storeis about Kublai Khan, the Mongolian emperor and grandson of Genghis Khan, who lived in a leather tent covered with ermine skins and who wore gold-covered leather garments. The Chinese at that time already had flexible tanned leather with vivid dyes, as well as lacquered and decorated leather.

Since the Middle Ages, the European craftsmen had tried to change the natural grain pattern of leather, to soften it or to eliminate it entirely. Several crafts were specialized in the creation and manufacturing of leather and its products, such as tanners, leather dyers, shoe makers, bag makers, belt makers, saddlers, and lace makers. This variety made it necessary to delineate the individual arenas of work, with everyone fighting for his special niche.

Container made from raw hide with engraved drawing, bone tools; Egypt, 4000 BC, © Deutsches Ledermuseum-Schuhmuseum Offenbach

For example, the bag makers were allowed to furnish their products with metal rings and buckles, whereas the pouch makers were not. The craft of belt making became a metal working business, and leather belts were only made by belt makers. The saddle making craft in particular underwent extraordinary changes. Because of the new industries of the 17th and 18th centuries, the saddle makers were doing upholstery work with chairs and sofas, appointed the growing number of carriages, and eventually manufactured suitcases and travel bags. The shoemakers had been responsible for the manufacture of vegetal-tanned leather apart from their own proper craft until the late Middle Ages. Around the 15th century the crafts of tanner and shoemaker split apart.

The manufacture of shoes was relatively easy to learn, as it did not require a large workshop and only simple and cheap tools were necessary. Because of this, the shoe making craft developed into one of the most numerous. The number of master craftsmen kept rising despite limitations and reached a climax in the 18th century. Large contracts for the army resulted in decisive changes in the organization of city craftsmanship. The limitations to the size of the shops were eased, and during the first half of the 19th century, the lucrative profession of storage master developed. He was allowed to keep a large amounts of leather in storage and produced for supply in a workshop that was separate from the craft shop. Due to the system of manufacture, the crafts were displaced, and the one-time shoemaker became a shoe repairman.

So much for some basic data and highlights of the history of leather. The real history of leather is the history of tanning.

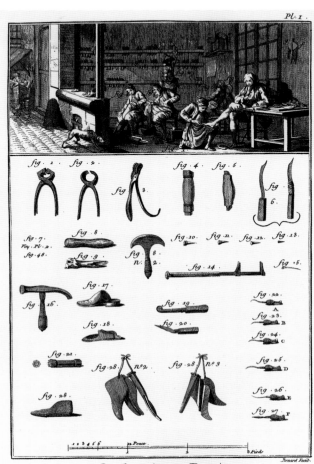

Leather manufacturing, shoe and boot maker workshop, tools, from: Diderot/d´Alembert, *L´Encyclopédie*

Tanning

The craft of tanning is one of the earliest lines of work of our ancestors because the search for methods to conserve animal skins is as old as the need of humans to clothe themselves.

Tanning and dyeing vats in the tanner´s quarter of Fès, Morocco

The History of Tanning

For a long time, the only kind of clothing was the skins that were taken from already dead animals, from scavenged remains or from hunting. But these trophies had little practical use because untreated skins become hard as wood or rot away. Around the end of the Early Stone Age, about 8000 BC, humans began to search for means and methods of avoiding this, often by rubbing fat substances into the raw hides. Using stone scrapers, they eliminated hair and flesh from the hides, and then softened them with bone marrow and animal brains or urine. For weeks they moved, kneaded, and rolled the raw hides, repeatedly impregnating them with fat, until the hides turned into durable, soft leather. This method can still be found in Asia, in countries close to the Arctic Circle, in America, and in South Africa.

Real leather, that is, durable, tanned animal skin, was first made in Egypt and Mesopotamia. The town of Gebelein in Upper Egypt was excavated by Ernesto Schiaparelli, where he unearthed a 5,000 year-old tanning shop. Not only did he find half-finished pieces of leather and skin, but tanning tools and shoots of Acacia Nilotica, which, without a doubt, provided the tanning compound. An analysis showed that, after all these thousands of years, the tanning compound content of the leather was still over 30 percent. But plant-based tanning was not the only method known to the Egyptians. The craftsmen knew much about tanning

Leather-making during the early Neolithic._ © akg-images

methods based on minerals and oils. Sesame oil for example, rich in unsaturated fatty acids, was imported from Syria. Leather had an important place in the life of Egyptians, and leather craftsmen were esteemed. Their leather products were widely distributed in the Land of the Nile. Garments, military equipment, musical instruments, sandals and shoes, containers for food, and, most importantly, all kinds of colored belts and bands were made from leather.

The use of alum, the basis of mineral tanning, was known in ancient Egypt, and the recipes for tanning solutions can be traced back to about 3000 BC. The grave of Tutankhamun, about 1550 BC, contained alum-tanned leather in a good state of conservation. For unknown reasons, tanning based on alum vanished, only to reappear centuries later, with slight changes, among the Hebrews, Scythes, Babylonians, Assyrians, Persians, Sumerians, Libyans, and Carthaginians. The alum-tanning method was known in the Roman Empire. The Romans had a very strong, tough leather for sandals (corium) as well as soft and supple leather named aluta (alum leather).

Tomb of Rekhmire, Thebes, 18th dynasty, 15th century BC. The tomb paintings on the walls depict work stages and tools used for the manufacture of leather sandals.
© akg-images/Erich Lessing

The peoples living in colder climate regions also tried to work with hides, particularly seal skins. With the Ulo knife and special stone scrapers, they scraped off the hair, tumbled the skins, and softened them in urine. The women used their teeth to masticate the hides until they became very soft. This tanning process, using fat, is one of the oldest tanning methods. Once they had prepared the hides in this way, they sewed them together using the tendons of seals or walruses.

Garments dating from the 5th century BC were found in Greenland, and were so well-preserved in the ice that the tanning method could be reconstructed. First, the hides' layer of fat was removed with clay and covered with a mixture of animal brain, liver, fat, and salt. The hides were then sewn together into a round tent, with needles made from bone or horn, and smoked over a open fire in the center of the tent. The effect of this smoke-tanning method was based on the active ingredient phenol, which is present in the smoke itself. Phenol is responsible for the black coloration of the moccasins that gave the Blackfoot Indians their name. The leather of these moccasins was smoked using the bark of oaks, the so-called black tanning process. Phenol is primarily responsible for the irreversible fusion of the tanning compounds with the animal skin fiber. It can also be found in today's plant-based and synthetic tanning solutions.

Tannery, from: Hamm, *Buch der Erfindungen*

Another rather primitive tanning method was widely used by other native peoples of North America. While many original cultures worked only the fleshy side of the hides, practicing smoke tanning), the Indians of North America worked the hides from both sides and achieved a fine buckskin for clothing, as well as a tough buffalo leather for tents. The tanners, most often women, used solutions made from sumac as the tanning agent. Sumac plants are poisonous trees or bushes with a high content of tanning compounds, so this tanning method is an early version of plant-based tanning.

The vegetal-tanning process can be documented since the Middle Bronze Age, about 2000 BC. Vegetal-tanning used primarily the bark of oak and beech trees as the tanning agent. In the old cultures of Asia, the gall nut with up to one-fourth of its weight consisting of tanning solution played an important role in the manufacturing of leather. By the end of the Bronze Age, the three main tanning methods had been developed: fat-tanning, vegetal-tanning and alum-tanning.

Native American women doing leather work, from: *Hamm, Buch der Erfindungen*

These three methods had been applied professionally since the 14th century in what is today's Europe. The tanning methods and the different animal skins result in very distinctive types of leather. Regarding the grouping of production techniques within the tanning craft, the common groups of Middle Europe are used:

1   The fat tanners provided waterproof leather by tumbling it with fat and fish oil.
2   The vegetal tanners manufactured saddles and harnesses, soles and shoe leather by tanning with oak bark.
3   The alum tanners produced the finer and thinner garment leather with alum and salt tanning.

The tanning houses can still be recognized because of their expansive buildings with workshops, storage rooms, cellar vaults, galleries and drying floors.

They were usually located next to a river or stream where water was available. Due to the serious pollution they caused, they were often located at the town's edge, where the river flows away from it. The tanners of Prague, for example, were branded as "stinkers" due to the process's strong odors.

Because of this, tanners were given certain areas and streets where they could work. Today, street names and old buildings remind us of the historic tanner's quarters.

Apart from having crafty abilities, the business of tanning required hard physical labor. Standing for extended periods of time in cold water, working the heavy hides, the strong odors they produced, as well as tanning solutions and residues often resulted in serious illnesses. Colds, rheumatism, and infections were typical job-related illnesses. However, the master tanners' wives were usually spared this fate. They were concerned with the sales at markets and leather banks. The tanners' children also had to contribute. They walked and trampled the spent vegetal tanning solutions into forms, which were subsequently dried and sold as fuel.

With the exception of children, only qualified workers were permitted in the tanning craft. In the 15th century, the apprenticeship lasted two to three years, qualifying the journeyman to serve the region. Receiving the master craftsman certificate required a high level of knowledge and skills. In the 17th century the admission to the craft was limited to sons of master craftsmen and in-law apprentices.

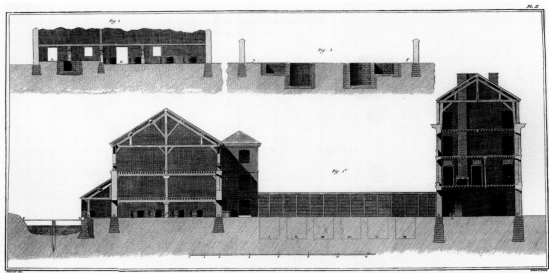

Tannery building, from: Diderot/ d´Alembert, *L´Encyclopédie*

Tanneur, Coupes Longitudinalle et Transversalle de la Tannerie.

When a tanner died, his widow often married an apprentice to keep up the business. The inheritance and handing over of trades and businesses developed very strong, family business traditions. Some tanner family trees can be traced back centuries, and the tanner's guild is among the oldest guilds. The guild's emblem is the fleshing knife, which is used on the fleshing block to remove the fat and flesh parts as well as the top skin and hair.

Until the beginning of the 17th century, the craft flourished in European cities. Around 1600, there were some 81 craftsman masters in Leipzig, and in Nördlingen there were some 152 in the year 1618. Starting in the 17th century, the tanning craft expanded to smaller rural towns and markets, and the sales of the city-based businesses consequently were diminished. The city-based tanner's situation was further complicated by a change in fashion. Garment leather was not sought in fashion at the end of the Middle Ages. Light wool fabrics and colorful printed calico, a fabric made from cotton, were now called for. As a result the focus of the leather trade 17th and 18th centuries turned increasingly tp upholstery for chairs and carriages, as well as for suitcases and other travel luggage.

The volume of leather production was regulated by the guilds until the 18th century, however, during the second half of that century, and following the technological progress, large-scale craft shops and manufacturing plants developed. They were able to buy raw materials at lower prices and could increase the number of tanning pits. Now, even untrained and, therefore, cheaper workers could work in leather production. The production technology did not change much, and the large tanning companies did not switch from pit tanning to barrel tanning until 1830.

From the 18th century onwards, leather was imported from Turkey, Morocco, Spain, and Hungary. North America provided a very cheap sole leather, which was smoke-tanned with the bark of the hemlock fir and called "red ghost" due to its red color and the feared competition.

Only recent history has provided essential improvements in the manufacture of leather, influenced by overseas trade and the industrial revolution. At the beginning of the 19th century, science was increasingly occupied with studying the tanning process. The use of quebracho wood and its tanning agent shortened the tanning process at the large plants to a maximum of eight weeks. One of the major breakthroughs, in 1858, was the development of chrome salts and the mineral tanning process they provided. The chrome-tanning method is still the foundation of the production of leather today. This method reduces the tanning process to a few hours. The leather would become much softer and more suitable for its applications. New machines, such as leather splitting machines, smoothing machines, and rotating tumbler barrels, made it possible to hire more and more untrained workers, each assigned a portion of the tanning task. The smaller, independent craft businesses were not able to withstand the pricing policy and had to close.

Fig. 275. Arbeiten am Schabebaum.

Working with the deflesher on the scraping block, from: Hamm, *Buch der Erfindungen*

Excursion: Morocco

Morocco was, and is, famous for its very fine, thin, soft leather of vibrant colors—so famous that its name is used to describe small leather articles. For example, the "Morocco" is a small leather-bound notebook. Not only small leather articles carry the name, but the entire leather goods industry, as well as the specialized retailers for bags and suitcases, are named "maroquinerie" in French. Morocco's large stock of cattle, including sheep, goats, and camels, as well as its many different native plants rich in tanning agents, have assured the success of its tanners. However, only a handful of tanners remain from what were originally over one hundred establishments. The Moroccan tanning industry is concentrated in the royal cities of Marrakesh and Fes, where the very archaic method of tanning can still be observed today.

Medieval tannery in Fes, Morocco

No signs of modernity can be seen at the Choura Tannery, located at the river Oued Fes. There is a horrible smell in the air. This world is immersed in death and resurrection, as the skins, after the slaughter and elaborate tanning processes, find a new life—in the form of leather. By transforming the skins into leather, the profession of the tanner acquires a symbolic and a social function as well. Leather workers are highly regarded people, and they belong among the most important craftsmen in Morocco. With the relatively high unemployment rate of the area, the well-paid traditional tanning profession is much sought after, despite the fact that the workers are usually finished by age 35 due to the extremely hard physical nature of the job. The job at the tannery demands much of them. With their bare feet, young men trample on the hides in the vats that are filled with concentrated tanning solutions or color brews—this permanent humidity causes them to have early rheumatism.

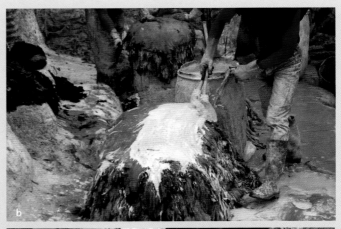

a Soaking the hides in the city´s
   waste water
b Workers putting a lime
   mixture on the hides
c Pulling the wool
d Tanning vats
e Large rotating washing drum
f Tanned hides drying on
   wooden racks

About one thousand men work at Africa's oldest and largest tannery in Fes. It was founded in the 11th century and is still run today according to methods from the Middle Ages.

Swaying donkeys, loaded with stinking hides that have previously been soaked in the waste waters of the city, but are otherwise untreated, run through the labyrinthine streets of the Souks, where no car fits in. They deliver the raw material for the tannery. The untreated hides of sheep, goats, cows, or dromedaries are piled several feet high at the tannery's entrance. A little further on, a few men are busy covering the flesh sides of the hides with a white-turquoise mixture based on lime, piling them up again when done. After five days in the glaring sun, the bare hide can be stripped of the hair and adhering lower skin layers. Rinsed in water, the bare hide is now freed from the mortal realm. They are tanned in white brick vats with a whitish liquid consisting of ammonia, pigeon excrement, wheatmeal, and salt. The caustic pigeon excrement is highly acidic and makes the leather soft. After five days in the tanning vat, where they are tumbled and flipped, the hides are put into a huge washing drum for six hours. Salt and flour are added to the rinsing water, which is replaced every half hour. Following this, the workers hang the now white leathers to dry for one week.

Now comes the dyeing process. Each week a different color is used for tanning. The tannery teams are adamant

Young man fulling the hides in the dye vat

about the fact that all of their coloring agents are natural and plant-based: bell pepper or red poppy dyes leather in bright red, rose dyes pink, henna dyes orange, henna mixed with sugar dyes black, indigo is used for blue, green from mint and pomegranate, and saffron dyes yellow. Saffron is the costliest of the dyes. The leather is tumbled with bare feet inside the vats with the dyes. The flesh side is now separated from the still adhering lower skin layers with continuously sharpened knives, and the thickness of the skin is evened out. Following this process, the leathers are left to dry for another 15 to 20 days on wooden drying racks. The saffron-dyed, bright yellow leathers are left to dry with the colored side down on top of a straw bedding.

Mountains of wool are building up at all the free spaces of the tanneries. This is "dead" wool which has been separated with the lime-shearing method. It has no further value for the Moroccan textile industry, so is used as filling material for mattresses.

Camels loaded high with hard, white or colored leathers transport the finished skins for further manufacturing in the small workshops of Medina. There, the leather is worked into babouches (a kind of slippers without heels), bags, or poufs.

With sharp knives, the flesh side of the skin is freed from the skin tissue

a   "Dead" wool
b   Saffron-dyed leathers
    drying on straw
c   Typical moroccan
    babouches

Histology of the Animal Skin

From the point of view of the tanner, the most important hides come from mammals, mainly from plant eaters, but also from omnivores like the pig. The composition of the hides is chemically and histologically about the same.

The skin/hide is the organ which covers the body and which makes it tough and impermeable to outside factors. It is an organ of evacuation and it regulates the body's water via perspiration. It is also a sense organ which can feel many things via its sensitive nerve system: differences in temperature, pressure, touch, and pain. And it can itch, too. Leather is skin-turned-durable, and it retains its primary characteristics even after tanning, particularly its breathability and elasticity.

The animal skin consists of about 65 percent water and 35 percent protein (collagen). Its high water content is a good medium for decomposing bacteria, and hence the water is eliminated almost entirely during the tanning process.

The animal skin consists of three layers: the outer skin or epidermis, the corium, and the connective tissue of the subcutis.

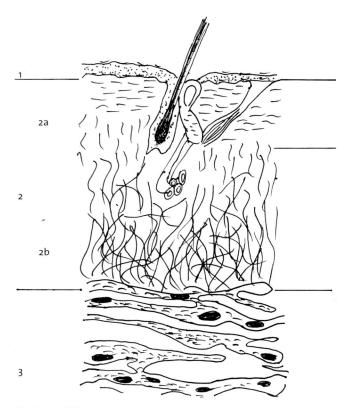

The Animal Skin

1 Epidermis with layers of horn and mucus
2 Corium with hair roots, tallow and sweat glands, and collagen fibers
2a papillary layer
2b reticular layer
3 subcutis connective tissue with flesh, blood vessels, and fat depositions

The epidermis itself is, in fact, the sensory and protective organ. It is the living part of the skin, as it renews itself constantly. It consists of a so called layer of horn and mucus and serves as a protection from bacteria and as a carrier of hair. Its thickness is only about one percent of the total skin. The epidermis is removed at the water workshop prior to tanning.

The tanner only utilizes the middle layer, the corium, for the production of leather. Its thickness is about 85 percent of the skin's total thickness. All its inherent characteristics are reflected in the tanned leather. The corium of almost all animals exhibits two defined layers: the papillary layer, just under the epidermis, and the reticular layer, shaped like a net. The latter one comprise an uneven knitting of thicker bundles of fiber, so the reticular layer provides toughness to the leather. The papillary layer (derived from papilla, a wart-like elevation) is broken up with the grooves of the hair roots and the openings of the tallow and sweat glands. The relation between the papillary and reticular layers is different for the various animal species. A goat hide consists of 35 to no more than 50 percent of papillary layer, a sheep hide up to 60 percent, and the skin of the domestic pig consists almost entirely of the papillary layer. The fiber network of the papillary layer gets denser and thinner towards the surface, ending with the grain membrane. The grain of leather receives its name from the typical hair grooves and sweat pores. By looking at the grain pattern, the origin of the leather can be determined. For example, pig leather is easily identified due to its rough grain pattern, which is due to its thick bristles.

Once the upper and lower skins are separated from the leather skin, it appears as a very smooth, milky-white membrane—the de-haired hide. The skin can be split horizontally along its entire surface due to its swollen state. This is how the grain-, middle- and flesh-split is obtained if the skins are relatively thick.

The lower skin or subcutis consists mainly of connective tissue and fat tissue, which mostly serves to thermally insulate the body, as a cushion against pressure, and as a storage facility for reserve nutrients. It is connected to the leather skin, without a clear separation between the two. The lower skin is not really durable and is removed entirely before the tanning process.

From Skin to Leather

Put simply, the following process happens during tanning: of the three layers, only the leather skin, the whitish corium, is used. Once boiled in water, the corium or de-haired hide turns almost entirely into glue. If left untreated, it dries out like horn. During drying, the individual fibers attach closely and bind together. If it is kept humid, bacteria destroy the organic matter. However, things are entirely different if the humidity is replaced with a tanning agent. It binds with the fibers, protects against decay and prevents the fibers from sticking together. Such are the conditions for the tanning of leather, and all tanning methods are based on them. The tanning agents, water-based solutions, get absorbed by the corium and bind irreversibly with the protein fibers. This physical-chemical process converts the hide into durable and tough leather.

Most hides today come from cows, calves, sheep, goats, pigs, and domesticated buffaloes. After slaughter, the hides are dried and usually conserved with salt for their trip to the tannery. The average-sized hide needs some 10 kg (20 lb) of salt.

Once the raw hide arrives at the tannery, a complex technical process is initiated which can be described, in a nutshell, as consisting of the following sixteen steps:

1 **Conservation:** raw hides and furs are salted for conservation
2 **Soaking:** watering, soaking, and cleaning removes dirt, rests of blood and fat, and the salt

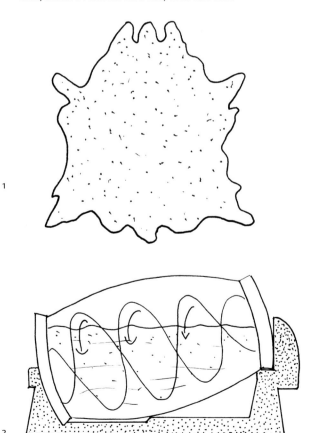

3   **Liming:** adding slaked lime and sodium sulphide in the rotating barrel removes the hair from the hide

4   **De-fleshing:** removal of remaining rests of flesh and fat with sharp knife-cylinders in the de-fleshing machine

5   **Equalizing:** with the knife-cylinders of a splitting machine the hide is evened out to a uniform thickness

6   **Pickling (loosening of fabric):** during this step, salt and acid are added into the rotating barrels to prepare the skin for tanning

7   **Tanning:** during the tanning process the skin fibers absorb the tanning agent

8   **Wringing:** cylinders press out the excess water

9   **Splitting:** depending on its thickness, the process of splitting divides the hide across its entire area into several layers. The leather is split with horizontally rotating knives through its fat layer (1). The resulting layers are called: 1. top layer, or grain split, 2. flesh split, 3. intermediary split (only present in exceptionally heavy hides)

10 **Folding, clinching:** the grain leather is evened out to a uniform thickness

11 **Neutralizing, dyeing and greasing:** the acid from the tanning process is neutralized. Leathers are grouped into dyeing batches and dyed. Adding fats to the solution results in the softness of the finished leather.

12 **Washing inside the tumbling barrel, wringing, and stretching:** the leather is stretched on a toggle frame

13 **Drying:** the vacuum drying process sucks out the humidity, while the convective drying method moves the leather on racks through ovens

14 **Milling:** in order to soften the leather after drying, it is milled mechanically

8

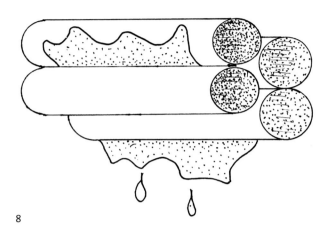

9

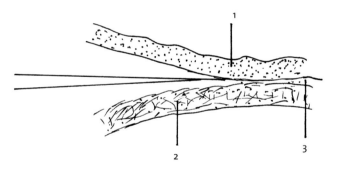

11

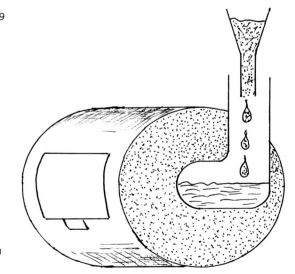

Fat-Tanning

15 **Finishing:** extremely thin layers are applied onto the leather. The leather gets its final appearance with priming, dyeing baths, top color layers, embossing, surface sanding, pressing or special grain effects.

16 **Final touches and quality control:** cutting of hide borders, measuring of its surface, quality control and sorting.

Leather does not loose its elasticity and smoothness after tanning, in fact, its natural toughness is augmented. The leather's properties depend on the tanning agents that are used. They are grouped into four kinds: fats, vegetal, mineral and synthetic tanning agents.

Tanning with fat is certainly the oldest form of modifying raw hides. It is usually done with fish oils and egg yolks, cow butter and linseed oil. This method is mostly used for the hides of wild animals such as stag, deer, chamois, or antelope, however, weak hides from cow, calf, goat, sheep, and split leathers are also tanned with this method.

The particular element of this process is the absence of tanning agents, as fats and fish oils are worked into the hide through the oxidation process. In order that the oils and fats can be better absorbed by the hide, the grain layer is removed together with the hair. The hide is painted with fish oil and kneaded for half a day to a full day with a tumbler. During the tumbling process the fish oils bind with the remaining water and permeate the cell structure. The tanning effect is due to the fact that the oils and fats absorb the oxygen from the air, oxidizing and becoming rancid. This is how the leather gets its milky-yellow color and its particular odor.

The superfluous fats are then removed with a solution of soda or pot ash. The leather is then washed, pressed, and smoothed using mechanical treatments. Window leather is a typical fat-tanned leather.

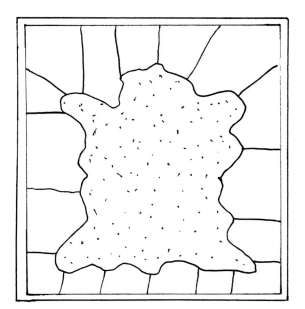

13

Vegetal- or Bark-Tanning

Various types of wood, bark, fruits, leaves, and roots have a high content of tannins and can be ground up and used for vegetal tanning. There are over 300 plant-based tanning agents, for example oak, beech, and fir trees, gallnut, chestnut, or extracts from tropical plants such as the bark tannin mimosa of the black acacia from Africa and Australia. The wood tanning agent quebracho is somewhat problematic as the quebracho extract is derived from the slow-growing quebracho rainforest trees.

Traditionally, vegetal tanning was performed using thin solutions in vats where the tanning agent was slowly absorbed by the skin—this type of tanning is also called pit tanning. This process could take at least six months and up to three years. Although this slow tanning process improved the quality of the leather, there was an eventual transition to speeding up the tanning, based on an economic point of view. The skins where turned inside large barrels filled with tanning extracts while heating the solution to 40 degrees Celsius (100 degrees Fahrenheit). The rotating barrels both knead and stretch the skins so the tanning agent is absorbed more quickly. After a few days the tanning process is completed. Although this type of treatment lowers the price of the leather, its fiber structure is looser when compared to pit tanning.

Vegetal tanning was the most important tanning method up to the middle of the 20th century and was later eventually replaced by chrome tanning.

Vegetal tanned leather is firm, not greasy, and can be shaped well while wet. It is suitable for work with punches and carvings. Some types of leather are not flexible and

Vegetal tanning, workshop with pit tanning, from:
Diderot/d´Alembert, *L´Encyclopédie*

Mineral- or Chrome-Tanning

maintain their shape even while being very thin. This firm vegetal tanned leather is suitable for tack and straps, belts, soles, briefcases, and hat boxes. However, there is also a rather greasy, soft, and matte vegetal tanned leather for furniture upholstery and bags.

Saffian is a well-known, fine colored leather tanned with sumac or gallnut. It has a very particular smell. The thin skins absorb the tanning agent quickly so the process takes only a few hours. In order to achieve a uniform absorption of the tanning agent, the wet skins are sewn together so that each one forms a watertight bag with only a small opening. The bags are filled with a highly concentrated sumac extract and inflated until all of its creases are eliminated. The opening is closed with a thread. The balloon-like shapes are placed into a large vat with hot water and a little sumac solution. After three hours of stirring, the tanning process is complete and the skins are hung from houses, rocks, or spread on the ground.

Tip: Take a scrap piece of vegetal tanned leather and cut it into two pieces. Moisten one of them. Take a punch iron or any tool to press both the dry and the wet leather. You will see how much easier it is to work with the moist piece.

Vegetal tanned leather can be recognized because of its particular smell. While at a leather retailer or shop, smell the different types and ask the retailer about the different tanning methods. You will quickly recognize vegetal tanned leather because of its special aroma.

And one more thing: vegetal tanned leather squeaks when it is rolled up. Other types of leather usually do not have this characteristic.

The white-tanning with alum is one of the oldest mineral tanning methods. It is particularly important that fat be thoroughly removed, which is why the tanners first placed the de-haired hides into the liming barrel, then rinsed and worked them with a blunt knife on the de-fleshing block. They would then be soaked again, tumbled and stretched. Only after being completely free of dirt, fat and lime would the tanners put them into the tanning solution, where they would receive several passes before being piled up in their wet condition and where they rested for one day. Then the leathers were dried. The tanning solution of white tanners consists of a specific solution of alum and salt in hot water. The clay of the alum penetrates the skin fiber, similar to alum which is used in textile dyes.

With inorganic tanning solutions, for example chrome salts, the tanning agent is mainly derived from associated hydro-complexes as caustic salts. The chrome salts are derived from chromite and turned caustic with caustic soda or lye. According to the manufacturers of modern trivalent chrome (III) salts, they are not harmful. The chrome-tanning method has replaced all other tanning methods due to its favorable properties. Some 85 percent of all leather is chrome-tanned.

The tanning takes place inside the tumbling barrels with an increasing concentration of the tanning agent. Depending on the thickness of the hide, this can take several hours. After this process the leather is left for a few days until the collagen has bonded with the chrome salts. Once the tanning is done, the leather is deacified and dyed.

A typical type of leather derived from mineral tanning is glacé leather. Zircon and aluminum are used as tanning agents.

Synthetic Tanning

Synthetically derived substances, so-called syntanes, are used for this type of tanning method. These are primarily phenols, which are used by themselves or in combination with plant-based tanning agents to convert animal skins into leather. The synthetic tanning agents provide certain properties to the leather. The chemical tanning agent Regulan GT 50, which is a glutardialdehyde tanning agent, makes the leather soft, permanently washable, and resistant against sweat. Regulan GT 50 is filling and apt for use in medical areas.

Recognizing the Tanning Method

The applied tanning method is important for the further treatment of leather. The easiest way to spot the tanning method is with the undyed leather, as each tanning agent colors the leather in its own specific way. If a leather has not been completely dyed, the proper tanning agent color can be seen at the cutting edge.

Leather tanned with fish oil and fat is light yellow to yellow. Vegetal-tanned leather can be yellow-brown, brown, or reddish brown, depending on the agent used. The burn test shows a colorless (white) ash. Vegetal-tanned leather squeaks when rubbed together. Chrome leather is green, blue-grey, or violet. A burn test shows a characteristic green ash. Glacé leather is white after the tanning process. Synthetically tanned leather is a golden yellow.

Tip: For a burn test, grab a small piece of leather with pincers and burn it with a lighter. Although leather does not burn, it glimmers. Place the burnt piece on a plate and study the ash, its color and consistency. Do this with an open window, there may be poisonous substances contained in the leather.

1.4 Dyeing

The dyeing of leather is likely as old as leather itself. When man began to wear animal skins, he soon tried to color them with the juice of plants. Perhaps the invention of vegetal tanning comes from this desire of adornment. It may well be that, while trying to dye animal hides with tree barks or other plants, it was first noticed that the animal skin changed its properties in the process, turning into "leather." Still today, tanners call the first treatment of the hide "pre-dyeing."

The oldest scriptures of the Bible report in the book of Exodus that the tabernacle (the tent which contained the Ark of the Covenant) was covered with red ram hides. During prehistoric times in Egypt, some 7,000 years ago, the dyeing of leather was fairly commonplace. The Egyptians took advantage of the properties of alum, which was combined with plant and animal extracts and yielded red, purple, and violet leathers. Solutions containing copper resulted in green tones; iron vitriol and tanning agents from acacia trees dyed blues and blacks. The oldest known pair of shoes (dated to 4000 BC) from a grave in Ghebelên shows clear evidence of green paint. The Greeks utilized the bark of the lotus tree as well as the root of the madder plant in order to dye leather. Around 600 BC, the Greek lyricist Sappho sang about colored leather in the following verse:

> "The feet are hidden by a colored strap
> beautiful lydian handiwork"

The Romans left us a comprehensive list of leather dyeing materials. They include kermes for red tones, saffron for yellow, wau (a kind of mignonette), and woad for blue, plus many more. The Roman's shoes and sandals were not only brown, they also wore black, light-blue, and green shoes. Red shoes were reserved for the emperor. His shoes were dyed with purple, the highly valuable dyeing compound of the single-walled mollusks (Murex and Purpurea).

Leathers of all colors

During the Middle Ages, it was primarily the glove which was the focus of a highly developed leather dyeing craft. Particularly during the 16th and 17th century in France, glove dyers had their heyday. The aristocrats wore gloves in the most eye-catching colors: reseda green, pink, and purple. The Huguenots who emigrated from France in 1685 brought their craft of leather dyeing to Germany and England.

Before the introduction of synthetic dyes, leather was dyed with similar dyes to those which were used with fabrics. Red was dyed with the Cochenille lice and with kermes, blue with indigo, green with green span, and yellow with saffron and yellow wood. The recipes depended on the tanner's experience and were kept secret. Up until about a hundred years ago, black top leather for shoes was dyed with beer soot, composed of five parts stainless iron filings and 25 parts of beer. Depending on the length of the dye bath, the color impregnated more or less deeply into the leather.

The purely craftsmanship-based tradition of leather dyeing was initially not influenced by the invention of synthetic dyes around the mid-19th century, however, the introduction of chrome-tanning changed the craft on a fundamental level. Chrome leather is very susceptible to dye right after tanning. The dye industry tested textile dyes for their aptitude for leather. The mixture of acidic and substantive dyes was discovered with respect to even chrome-tanning.

Leather does change its own color depending on the tanning agents. Different colors are achieved by either placing the hides in rotating barrels with dye or by brushing or spraying on the dye. While in past the dyes were natural compounds, today the dyeing is done with anilin dyes. Anilin is a synthetic oil produced from the tar of hard coal, colorless and odorless, yet very poisonous. Even today the use of water soluble transparent dyeing processes is called anilin dyeing, although the component anilin is no longer part of it, due to environmental concerns. The dyeing with anilin conserves the natural character of the leather. The tanned leather is either dyed in the barrel or with an even spray-on process. The grain pattern is completely conserved. Anilin leather belongs among the finest quality leathers. But Anilin-dyed leathers are more delicate than painted leathers. Their heat resistance is low, which has to be taken into account while working them (for example, when ironing).

During the protein dyeing process, casein, a protein binding agent, is added. This is how leather gets its beautiful color brilliance. But this dyeing method allows for only very thin layers to be built up. They form a very thin but intense color layer. This layer would be too thin for leather with a flawed grain pattern. In that case, dyes based on plastics are used. The casein is replaced by polymers and applied with an airbrush. Over 70 percent of all top leathers are dyed this way. The colors must not flake off or rub away at areas of stress.

Another method for coloring leather is by lacquering. This method provides a high brilliance to the leather and is therefore very much subject to fashion tendencies. The leather is prepared by slightly roughing up the grain. Nowadays, the use of polymer lacquers is more and more common. The lacquering process is fast and the resistance to loss of brilliance and kinking is good.

After dyeing, the leather is dried. In former times, the wet leathers were put out to dry on wooden poles in the warm air. Today, they are dried in a vacuum dryer stretched on a rack.

The color and light resistance is important for the quality of the leather. Light resistance can only be determined after direct sunlight incidence. A leather that is little light resistant will become lighter, while vegetal-tanned leather will get darker.

1.5   **The Grain Pattern**

The grain side of leather is the smooth side, with its typical small grooves of the papillary layer. Because of its look and ease of care, it is usually worn outside. The fleshy side of leather is the rough, dull side, the reticular layer.

The grain pattern is determined by incisions and holes of hair, wool, and pores, as well as feathers and scale attachments. Their shape and their relationship with each other form the characteristic look of the grain side. A calf has a finer and smoother hide than a cow. Hence, its pores are significantly smaller and have a smaller diameter than those of the cow. The pores are located close together at irregular intervals and look like someone punched them at an angle with a sharp object. Depending on the age, species, and gender, many intermediate patterns exist, up to the coarse pattern of mature cows.

The horse's distribution and shape of pore exits is similar to those of the cow, though they appear to be even less regular. The pores are also of different sizes, the small ones belong to the undercoat, the larger ones belong to the top coat with its guard hair.

The goat has regularly spaced pores of undercoat and guard hair next to each other. Two to five guard hairs are placed in a half-moon shape in a row, while behind them there are four to eight guard hairs in the next row—this is the typical grain pattern of goats. The size of the pores can vary with age and species.

The guard and undercoat hair is not ordered into strict groups with sheepskin. The pores run in different undulating lines. They pierce the skin at a right angle. Since wool can grow strongly undulated, corkscrew-like, as well as densely and smoothly, its pores can have very different sizes.

The grain pattern of the pig can be recognized because of the large diameter of the pores as well as their large distance to each other. The typical arrangement is three bristles arranged as a triangle. Also, the bristles have grown through the entire thickness of the leather, which means that the leather skin of a pig consists entirely of the papillary layer.

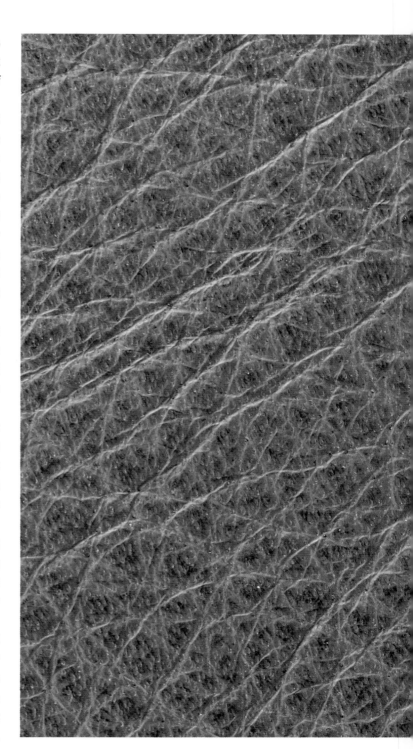

Cattle grain pattern

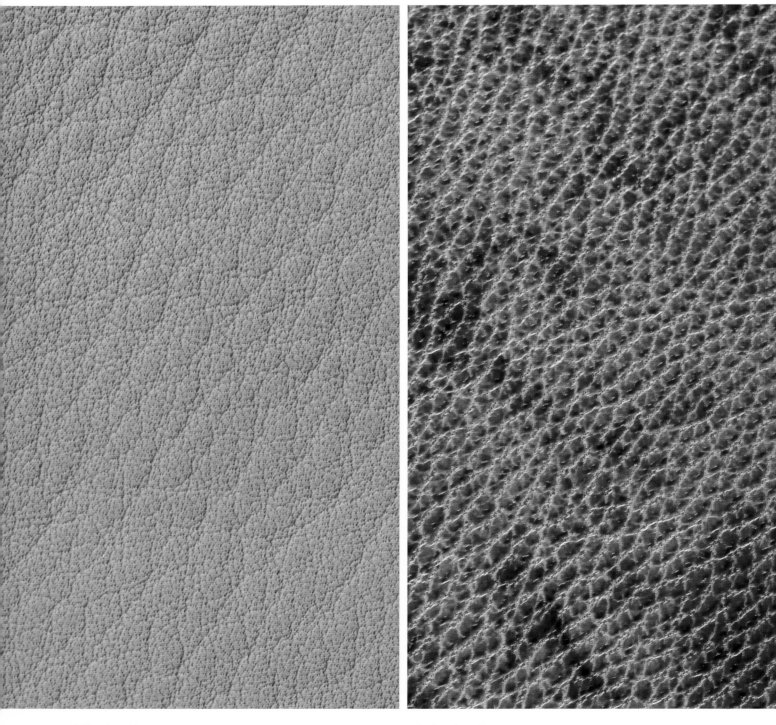

Calf grain pattern

Goat grain pattern

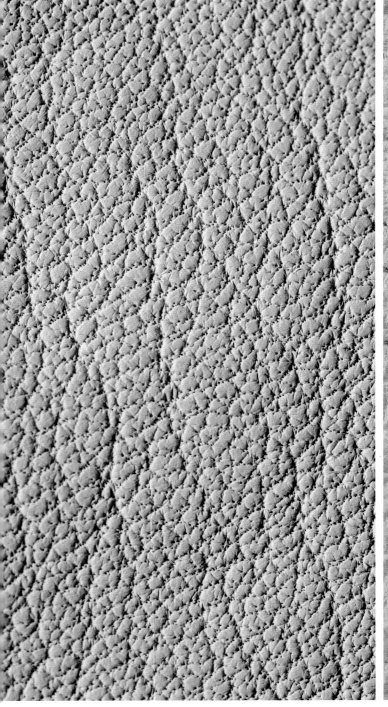

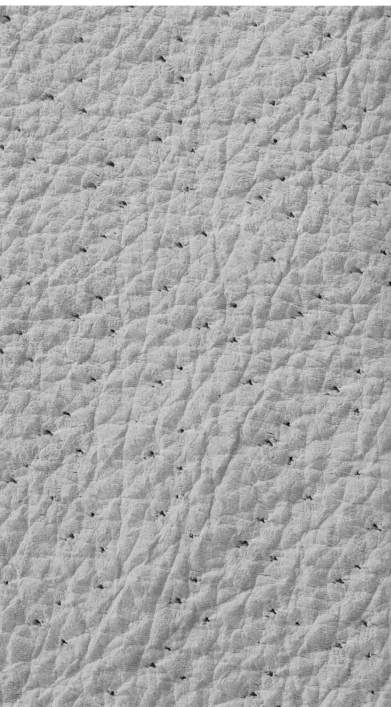

Sheep grain pattern

Pig grain pattern

Leather as Material

Leather Flaws

Damage to the skin has a disadvantageous effect on the finished leather. Leather flaws are categorized according to their location and appearance. There are many possibilities. Even simple skin flaws can lower the value of leather significantly. Damage, such as cuts from barbed wire, burn marks, thorns, parasites, or skin diseases, lowers the quality of the leather. Additionally, the faulty skinning or wrong conservation, the process of splitting, tanning, and dyeing can result in flawed grain, cuts, nicks, and above all, thin patches that can tear apart easily.

Apart from the mentioned leather flaws, the look of leather, meaning its grain pattern, the even dye, and the formation of stains, as well as the haptics (the inner fiber construction), serve as criteria for determining its quality. A skin can consist of very solid, well-structured, almost hard leather and still have unbelievably soft patches. This mix is not good at all when you are dealing with a leather jacket!

When purchasing leather, it is very important to touch the leather on both sides and to inspect it carefully; it is advisable to hold the piece of leather against a light source to spot the smallest of holes.

Leather Properties

Most of the properties of leather today are still determined by checking the leather physically, with the human senses. It may be a bit subjective, but even material testers with chemical or physical investigation methods first check the leather's exterior composition.

Part of these properties is the tensile strength, which is about 2.5 kg per square millimeter for good leather. Chrome-tanned leather has more tensile strength and is more tear-resistant than vegetal-tanned leather.

Another property is its waterproofness. Because of its special fiber composition, leather can absorb vapor within its fibers and transport it. Moreover, it can deposit and bind many substances which are given off by the human body. Good leather should not absorb more water than half its dry weight. Leather takes form under the influence of humidity from the human skin and adjusts to the body's movements. If the fat content is high, the water content is correspondingly lower. This assures the comfort of wearing leather garments. But its insulation properties also play an important role for garments as well as shoes; it protects against cold as well as against heat.

The fineness and evenness of its grain are further points in its classification. The skin of younger animals is thinner and less damaged than older hides. Grip, texture, and elasticity are also important criteria. Loose leather is soft and nimble and therefore not very durable. A simple test shows the leather's composition: taking a piece of leather, fold grain side against grain side. If it can be folded easily and the fold does not resist too much, then it is not very good as to tensile strength. Really grippy leather is dense and not easy to fold. The fold also disappears immediately and should leave no trace on the leather. Good, durable leather (for example top leather for shoes) can be folded ten to twenty million times before breaking. And, of course, it should not loose its form, either. Goat velours are particularly prone to this.

Leather Types

The tearing-strength of good leather is very high, which is important with garments worn close to the body, particularly the seam areas.

The firmness or strength denotes the resistance of leather to shape-changing outer forces. If the fiber bundles are particularly tight together, then great force must be exercised to move them or to tear them apart. The distribution of the firmness across the entire surface is shown in the firmness topography.

The parts with a denser line pattern denote a high firmness, while the outer and less dense areas are less firm. Lower quality leather and split leather generally have a poor tearing resistance.

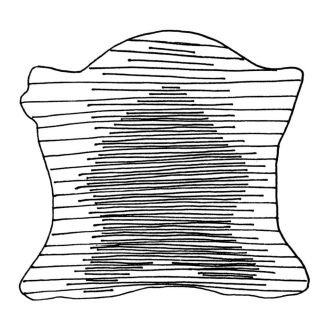

strength topography

All leather is not equal. The different animals provide leather which is typical for each animal species. But tanning, intended use, and equipment yield many kinds of leather whose look and properties differentiate them from each other. These properties are used to determine leather for garments (jackets, pants, shirts, and above all, shoes) and items of daily use (bags, furniture upholstery and riding equipment, or tack).

Every leather has two sides: the grain side, where hair used to grow—easily discernible because of the presence of pores, and the fleshy side, the inner and rougher side. Thick hides are split before tanning, resulting in grain splits (the upper part of the skin), and flesh splits (the lower part of the skin). All split types are worked to become leather. The finished leathers can be put into two large groups:

1   The grain leather is processed to become smooth leather, nappa or, slightly sanded, nubuck leather, and it represents the largest of the groups. The natural grain pattern is conserved.

2   The split and fleshy sides of leather are used for making suede and velour in its many variations.

The naming of leather is either according to the animal from which it originates, according to the manufacturing method, according to its use, or according to its particular characteristics.

It is almost impossible to compile a complete list of all types of leather. I will therefore concentrate on the most common types of leather.

A

Anilin leather: traditional term for leather which has been dyed with soluble, transparent dyes, without any colored top layer. The original anilin dye was produced from tar, but due to health concerns, it has not been in use for decades. The grain pattern lies bare and exhibits the most natural look of all types of leather. Anilin leather is a very high-grade grain leather with a soft, skin-like surface.

Antique leather: smooth leather which can originate from several different animals. It is worked to obtain an old or vintage look by dyeing, printing or spraying. The treatment of its surface resembles a leather patina. Antique leather is blank leather with deep embossed grooves and used for furniture and vehicle upholstery. Sometimes the raised areas are slightly sanded.

B

Box calf: a chrome-tanned calf top leather, usually dyed black with anilin, suitable for light, fine shoe top leather, bags, and leather goods, with tight grain patterns.

C

Calf Leather: derived from male or female animals (up to one year old) which are fed exclusively with milk. Calf leather is easy to spot because of its densely arranged, thin hair grooves. Its fine grain determines its further use (for example, as top leather for shoes, bags, etc.). Calf hides measure about 0.7 to 1.7 m² (7 to 18 ft²) and weigh about 12 kg (26 lb).

Chamois leather: also called "deer leather", although it includes sheep, lamb, roe, gams, goat or kid. It is fat-tanned and split, or has a sanded grain. Due to the complete absence of the papillary layer and the grain, it is particularly soft. Chamois is often used as washing and window leather.

Chevreau leather: a chrome-tanned goat leather (French: chevreau = young goat) with very fine and delicate grains. All anilin colors are used to dye this leather, and it is also manufactured with high-gloss top colors as well as embossed with patterns. Gold and silver chevreau comes from high-gloss to satin-matt. It is used for shoes and bags.

Coated leather: in order to be called "leather", the coating can not exceed one third of the total leather thickness. Mostly split leather is coated. The grain is artificially embossed.

Cow leather: due to their large size, cow or bull hides are mostly used for making clothing and for upholstery.

A cow hide weighs on average some 30 kg (65 lb) and measures from 2 to 6 m² (20-60 ft²). Jackets, pants and furniture upholstery can be sewn together without too many extra seams. Bovine leather is also great for bags because of its tensile strength. The grain pattern shows an even distribution of pores, the fibers on the flesh side are coarse. The best section of the hide is the back, which has an even thickness. Cow leather can be thin and light as well as very tough and heavy, depending on how much leather has been split away.

Crumpled leather: a thin, soft leather (usually split leather) with a crumpled, flexible and soft lacquer coating. Crumpled leather is easy to clean.

D

Deer leather: fat-tanned strong leather derived from deer. Due to the fat tanning it is extremely soft. Usually used as suede.

F

Fish leather: a very interesting skin due to its patterns and pigmentation, mostly used for shoes and bags. Fish skins are tanned just like other hides. The shiny surface of the ray skin is particularly noteworthy, as it concentrates towards the center much like mother-of-pearl.

Full grain leather: a vegetal-tanned cow leather mostly tanned in pits, with an even fiber structure and thickness. Due to its fat content of five to ten percent it is very hard. Full grain leather is particularly suited for bag making and furniture, which is frequently abused. A strong leather that can be worked with open edges.

Full leather: un-split, thick leather. Top layer and split layer are not separated.

G

Glacé leather: a shiny smooth leather (glacé means shiny), often from a young goat, prepared on its grain side. Usually it stays white or is dyed on the grain side. Intensive

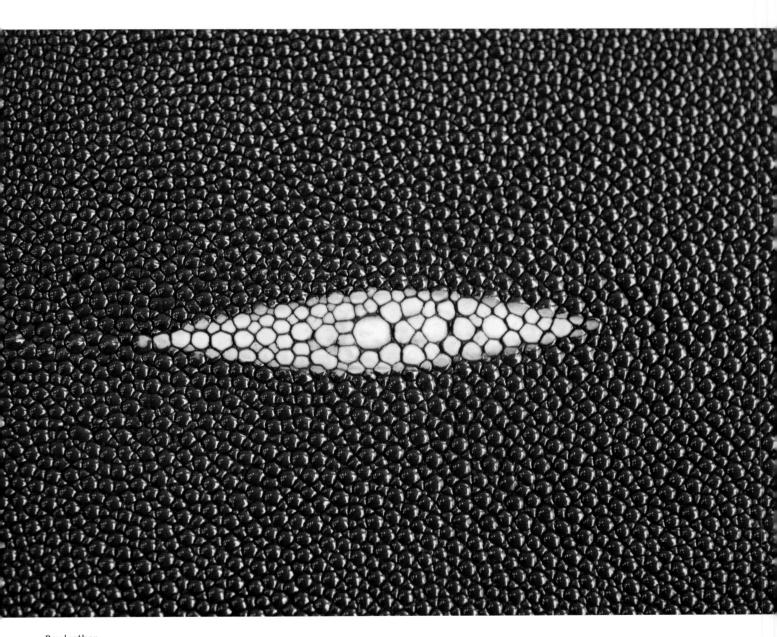

Ray leather

de-fleshing, pickling, and a special tanning method—usually with alum, flour, and egg yolk—provides softness. Due to its high tensile strength it is particularly suited for gloves.

Goat leather: denser and with a closer fiber pattern than sheep leather. It is both tough and soft, with a fine grain. The typical grain pattern consists of semicircular top coat hair grooves running diagonally towards the center. It also exhibits a marked spine, which can be observed in particular with parchment. Goat leather can be recognized due to its narrow shape, in contrast to the broad outline of sheep hides. Goat leather without a top color coating tends to stretch and loose its shape, which is why it is not well suited for clothing worn close to the body.

H

Horse leather: this leather has two main sections: the back, with dense, fine connecting tissue at both sides of the top line, and the neck, which is surprisingly long when compared to a cow.

K

Kangaroo leather: particularly high tear resistance, hence it is used mostly in sports.

L

Lacquered leather: usually split leather, either lacquered or covered with foil, resulting in a mirror-like smoothness and brilliance. Lacquered leather is stiff and practically without flexibility, waterproof and easy to clean.

M

Morocco leather: a particularly strong leather with a rough grain. Derived from the North African (moroccan) goat, or cape goat. This leather is usually worked like saffian leather, which has a finer grain.

Turkey foot

Snake skin—python

N

Nappa leather: a sub-type of anilin leather, which can originate from the following animals: cow, calf, horse, sheep, goat, lamb, or pig. Nappa leather is dyed through and its surface is finished, meaning, the pores are closed with many very thin layers and are therefore protected against dirt and moisture. This is a full-grain, smooth, grippy, tissue-soft and elastic leather.

Nubuck leather: made from fine-grained calf or cow hides with pure and error-free grains. The hides are chrome-tanned and deep-dyed. The velvet-like surface of nubuck is achieved by light sanding of its grain side. Just like velvet, the trace of a finger is visible. Nubuck is a typical suede.

O

Ostrich leather: particularly durable leather, easy to recognize because of its little knots at the spine.

P

Parchment: un-tanned skin from calf, goat or sheep. The hides are de-haired and de-fleshed and evened out via splitting. The hides are stretched on racks and dried, oiled, greased and flattened. Parchment and transparent leather are identical, except for the former's filling with color pigment.

Peccary leather: grain leather from the hides of free-roaming South American peccaries (a type of wild boar), dyed with anilin, exhibits a thin cover layer. Peccary is usually used for exclusive and noble men's clothing.

Pig leather: pig skin is traversed at an angle by the bristles, down to the fat layer. This causes a higher permeability when compared to other leathers. The bristles are placed in triangular patterns, fairly widely separated. Pig hide can be easily spotted because of its large grain with large pores. The skin consists entirely of the papillary layer and exhibits significant structural differences between the core pieces and the flanks. Extremely soft pig velour is used for leather shirts, vests, dresses, and jackets, and it is the cheapest of all leathers.

R

Reptile leather: crocodiles, lizards and snakes (all from farms nowadays) have horn-like warts on the top layer of their leather skin. The horn-like layer tends to increase with age, so the hides of younger animals are preferred. The skins are tanned and made flexible with a special process. Reptile leather keeps its shape very well. The different reptile species can be recognized because of their typical scale patterns. Reptile leather is mostly used for luxury articles.

S

Saffian leather: a vegetal-tanned goat leather, often from New Zealand stock with healthy grain and additional manual treatments to bring out its naturally small grain. Saffian is a hard, tough and very durable material, for example for book covers. Genuine saffian leather can be recognized due to its typical squeaking.

Semi-anilin: in between anilin and nappa leather, combining the advantages of both leather types.

Sheep leather: an interwoven fiber tissue with a lot of embedded fat. This causes double-layering, which results in a high propensity to tear. Sheep skins can be recognized by their large number of unevenly spaced hair grooves. Unlike goat skins, they remain visible after splitting the hide. The hide is characteristically rather wide, which is beneficial for its use. Sheep leather is commercialized as nappa or velour leather and is predominantly used for clothing.

Split leather: due to the splitting of the grain layer, split leather is coarse on both sides. Usually the split layer is finished. The distinction is made between coated split leather and split velour.

Suede: general term for leather with a velvet-like, rough finish. Usually grouped into:

1 grain-side worked leather such as nubuck
2 flesh-side worked leather such as goat velour
3 grain- and flesh-side worked leather, like pig and chamois
4 split full-grain leather

T

Transparent leather: just like parchment it is not a real leather because it has not been tanned. After de-hairing and de-fleshing it is stretched and rubbed with glycerin while drying.

Turkey leather: tanned and dyed turkey legs are used for appliqués or for watch wristbands.

V

Velour leather: the fleshy side is delicately sanded and obtains a velvet-like surface. Leather with damaged grain can be used for velour. The velour fiber of cows is coarse, while it is significantly smoother for calf and goat.

W

Wild animal leather: general term for leather derived from free-roaming animals such as elk, deer or gams. It is usually fat-tanned and the grain is completely split off.

Ostrich leather with its characteristic knots

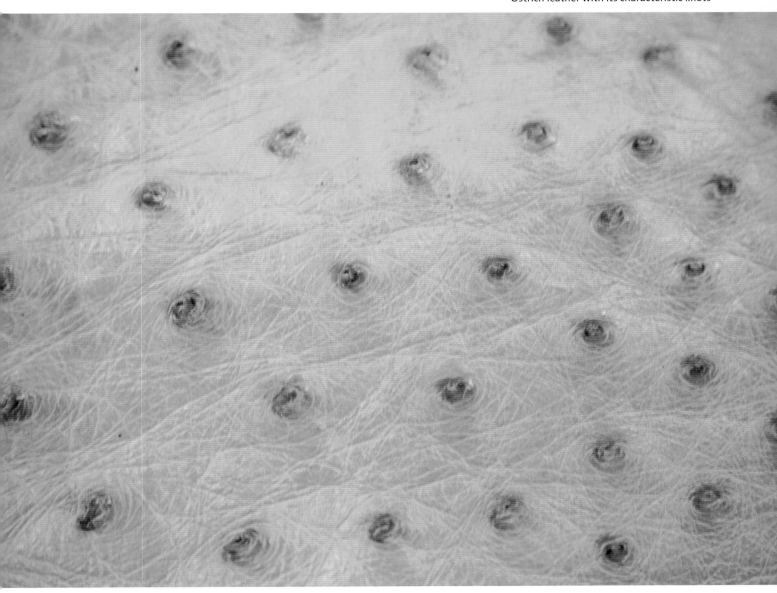

Leather Qualities

Unlike fabrics, leather is not manufactured on a loom and hence it is not as even and smooth as woven fabrics. There are many factors which contribute to the differences in quality. They include above all the age of the animal, its feed, the time of year of slaughter, and the climatic circumstances during its lifetime.

There are no standardized quality features within the leather industry. Price is determined by kind, size, and visual quality of the leather. The latter criterium is mostly determined by the existence of damages to the hide. Holes, thin patches, and staining are not desirable features, so leather should always be held against a light source and checked for errors before purchasing it. Leather is categorized into groups like 1, 2, 3, 4, or A, B, C, D ... However, these classifications do not reflect the leather's qualities regarding its wearability, they only indicate the usable part of the hide. Even the best quality leather is not flaw-free, as leather is a naturally growing material with individual properties.

With more and more experience, it becomes easier to tell good from bad leather. Strong brilliance indicates a thick cover lacquer layer, or easy maintenance. However, first impressions can be misleading: calf leather, in particular, is pressed to brilliance with large cylinders. By graining, that is, kneading, rolling, and massaging, the natural grain of the leather reappears and the leather becomes soft and matt.

One should not expect that leather will lie completely flat like fabrics, since it is derived from a three-dimensional form (the animal body's cover) and transformed into a two dimensional form. This process yields the soft, wrinkled, and elastic section from the flanks as well as the even, strong, and most stable part from the animal's back. This needs to be considered when laying out the cut patterns.

In this context it should be mentioned that leather has increasingly changed to become a cheap consumer article. Demand has increased very remarkably, and the result of this are environmental damage, bad working conditions at the tanneries, and the deficient quality of leather. Much of the leather hitting the market today is not a natural product anymore. After all, it consists of 20% tanning agents, dyes, and production materials that can cause allergies and skin rashes, for example in the case of new furniture leathers gassing off. Good leather retailers can be consulted to assure that you purchase a natural product which can be worn directly on the skin.

Classification

Leather hides do not have a uniform thickness and stiffness. The back is the densest section with the highest tensile strength, called the bend, or double butt if referring to both sides. It is the best part of the hide. The neck towards the top follows. It consists of shoulder, neck, head, and cheek sections. Next to the bend and neck are the sides, consisting of the belly and leg sections. The sides have a loose consistency and are therefore very soft, wrinkled, and elastic.

1   Neck
2   Front leg
3   Belly
4   Hind leg
5   Core
6   Spine
7   Flank

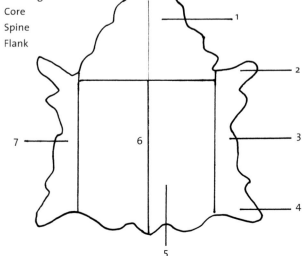

Purchasing Leather/Delivery Forms

The "grip" of leather plays a determining role in making a decision to purchase. Apart from its smell, look, and color, leather gives a direct feedback to touching it. Time should be taken when purchasing leather to test its characteristics and hold the selected piece against a light source. You should consult with the leather dealer about qualities and types of leather.

Tip: how do you spot synthetic leather?

Leather imitations consist of a textile fiber compound which is coated with plastics. They can resemble the real grain patterns to a remarkable degree, and some finished products make it difficult to spot the difference at first sight. Even the smell can be misleading. However, a magnifying glass can be used to look at the pores in detail: is the grain imprinted or are there real grooves and holes present? The burn test shows that synthetic leather burns with a boiling, stinking smell which leaves a hard residue, while leather does not burn, it only glimmers.

All haired raw skins from small mammals such as calf, goat, sheep, and deer used to be called pelts if their size was between 0.5 and 1.2 m² (5-12 ft²), while the skins of larger animals, including reptiles, were called hides. Today, these terms have been mixed up. The skins which are smaller than 0.5 m² (5 ft²) and which are skinned as a sleeve are called bellows, often from rabbit. Large, raw hides from cows or horses are split longitudinally to produce qualitatively sound leather. They are called sides, or sections. Hides and pelts in one piece are characterized by the shape of the animal body.

The size of a piece of leather is important when dealing with the cut. The larger the surface, the more advantageous for the layout, and the less clippings. The smaller the surface, the more difficult the layout and the higher the cutoff.

Size comparison of hides: goat on top of pig on top of a cow side

Leather is sold by the square foot or square meter, which is indicated on the backside of the leather. Each tanner works with his own size classification system, depending on the calibration of his machine. Usually, the small hides from sheep or goat are measured in square feet, and the larger hides from cow and horse in square meters. Thick and heavy cow hides are sold by weight.

One square meter equals about 11 square feet.

$1 m^2 = 100 dm^2 = 10.76 ft^2$
$1 ft^2 = 0.0929 m^2 = 30.48 cm \times 30.48 cm$

Goat and sheep hide: approximately 5–12 ft²
Pig hide: approximately 7–16.5 ft²
Calf hide: approximately 0.8–1.4 m²
Cow hide (sides): approximately 1.2–2 m²

The measurements given for commercially available cut patterns are in meters or centimeters, as they are intended for indicating the use of material for garments. However, leather is sold in square meters. For this reason, the material needed must be converted to square meters before purchasing leather.

The price of leather is determined by its quality and its type. Cow leather is usually sold as a complete hide or as a half side. Smaller leathers can only be purchased as complete pieces or as cutoff. For smaller leather works or for patchwork, leather residuals or rejected pieces with few usable sections are suitable. Also, leathers with dye defects are great for creative and budget-oriented projects.

Next to the size, elasticity plays an important role. The direction of minimal stretch indicates its highest tensile strength and needs to be taken into consideration when laying out the cuts. Existing cut patterns should be brought along when selecting leather, so make sure that it is large enough. It is often difficult to buy more leather after the fact, as the coloration can vary significantly between pieces.

The following is a conversion example for two meters at a pattern width of 140 cm.

1   Calculate how many square meters are contained in the particular pattern width (here, 1.4 m2).
2   This figure (1.4 m2) is multiplied by the number of necessary meters of length:
    2 x 1.4 m2 = 2.8 m2
3   Add to this number about 15 percent for cutoff and placement:
    15% = 2.8 m2 x 0.15 = 0.42 m2
4   Adding the two results in the required number of square meters:
    2.8 m2 + 0.42 m2 = approximately 3.2 m2

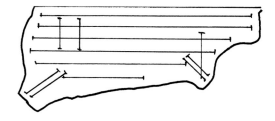

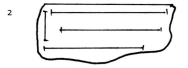

Direction of least stretching
1   Chrome cow leather
2   Chrome pig leather

Leather Storage

The most important characteristics of leather, such as elasticity, softness, and flexibility, are conditioned by a certain humidity content of the leather. Hence, it is important to store leather correctly. It should not be stored next to heating installations. Direct sunlight should be avoided as well, as the rays of the sun can bleach and stain the leather with time.

Leather hides are grouped in like color batches and placed one on top of the other, the lowest hide with the grain side towards the top, all others with the fleshy side up. When rolling up the hides, the grain side faces outwards and maintains tension. Only the outermost or lowest hide faces with its grain side inwards around the other hides, for protection. These rolls are stored lying flat on shelves.

The place of storage should be cool (5-15 degrees Celsius, or 40-60 degrees Fahrenheit) and not too dry nor too humid. A relative humidity of 50-70 percent is optimal.

Leather Care

Leather is among the fabrics that requires little care, due to its modern tanning and finishing technologies. However, if leather is to keep its positive characteristics, it needs to be taken care of appropriately. You need to know the type of leather you are dealing with. A little experiment should precede every session of leather care: put a drop of water on an unobtrusive part of the leather and observe carefully. If the spot gets a dark rim, then the leather is a high-absorption, delicate leather like anilin or nubuck. Leather with a light lacquer or top finish is easier to maintain.

Leather is tanned animal skin, and if not covered by a waterproof layer of lacquer (like lacquer leather) it is porous, breathable, and permeable. These are advantageous characteristics concerning its comfortable wearability, but the disadvantages are that leather attracts dirt and grease. Leather care should not only protect from dirt but provide a lasting usability.

Each session should be preceded with a lengthy cleaning of the leather, to get rid of dirt and remnants of old care materials. The purpose of leather care is to return it to its pristine condition, eliminate signs of use, and provide it with dirt and water-rejecting products. Most types of leather require only a surface treatment which provides longevity to the leather if applied regularly. Only few leathers such as high-performance leather (used for trekking boots) require that the care agent be absorbed by the leather.

According to its use, these care products are either for smooth leather or for suedes. The care of smooth leather involves a larger number of products that are divided according to their type and composition. There are leather care products with a surface action, such as shoe polish, leather sprays, or cleaning emulsions, which beautify the leather surface and protect against dirt and humidity. There are also care products with a depth effect, including leather oils, waxes, and greases, which are intended to maintain the smooth consistency of leather as well as to improve their water resistance.

Anilin leather should be regularly wiped with a soft cloth to eliminate dust. In case of more intensive soiling, use neutral soap and warm water to wipe large sections with a soft cloth.

Nappa leather is cleaned by carefully wiping its surface with a neutral cleaning agent. Care should be taken not to wet the leather thoroughly. After drying at room temperature, wipe the leather with leather care cream and polish with a soft cloth.

The above mentioned care products and materials are not suited for the care of suedes like velour, nubuck, or chamois. No fats, waxes, or oils are used, as they make the surface sticky and stain it. A preventive care is to spray them with waterproofing products, where a thinly aerosolized agent is applied to the leather. This makes it possible to treat very delicate types of leather evenly without staining. It is important to maintain the correct distance between the spray can and the leather. Before its treatment, the leather surface should be cleaned by brushing it gently.

Dust and loose dirt on suede can be eliminated with a vacuum cleaner. To get rid of large dirt patches or fatty patches, use a fine wire brush or sand paper, then vacuum off the dirt. There are special erasers which are suitable in particular for light-colored suedes.

Leather should be washed only if its type and label says so. Special chemical cleaning of leather is only recommended if the label states this. Nevertheless, there is always the option of leaving the care of leather garments in the hands of specialized personnel. Special cleaning shops take care of the cleaning and waterproofing, and can even apply a color refreshening. In any case it is good advice to check out the care and maintenance issues when purchasing leather.

Leather goods in general

Leather items are regularly wiped with a soft cloth to get rid of dust. Generally, all types of leather are finished with a protective surface coating. Care is only begun after the first stained patches appear. Use a moistened cotton rag with warm water and carefully wipe the leather. If this is not enough, try with a commercially available cleaning product. Always test care products on an unobtrusive patch first! Apply the care product quickly and over a large surface to avoid the formation of borders and clouds, and never apply it directly onto the leather but use a cloth to spread it across the leather. When your are done, do a finishing polish. Leather articles are maintained in longer intervals.

Leather furniture

Do not apply solutions like stain cleaners or alcohols or gasoline, nor waxes or shoe polish. Instead, clean occasionally with soapy water, then wipe off and polish with a dry wool rag.

It is important to follow the product instructions with respect to furniture care products. You can check the color properties of furniture leather by moistening a white and soft cloth with a little of the product and rub it onto an unobtrusive part of the leather. If the cloth changes in color, the product is not suitable. Furniture covered with anilin leather must be protected from direct sunlight!

Leather shoes

The best method to remove dry dirt on shoes is to brush it off. If necessary, the shoes can be wiped with a moistened cloth, which conserves breathability. Use shoe care products sparingly, and from time to time freshen them up with leather care finishing products. They resemble shoe polish, but are harder and more color intensive.

Unlike leather furniture and bags, shoes should get their first care treatment right after purchasing them, as you might catch the first rainy day just after buying them. Shoes intended for intense performance, like trekking boots, should be waterproofed from time to time. Ventilate and change the shoes regularly.

Leather clothing

When leather clothing gets wet, hang it on a shaped hanger at normal room temperature. It is not recommendable to dry leather clothing quickly with a heater or in sunlight, as the leather might turn hard and brittle.

Rain stains are difficult to treat, especially on smooth leather. The garment can be held over hot vapor, then dried and, if possible, greased.

If the garment is creased, it can be ironed. Set the iron to its lowest temperature and use a dry cotton or silk cloth between leather and iron. Test first on an unobtrusive section.

2

Tools and Techniques

Awls

2.1 Tools and Implements

There is no need for either many or large tools in order to work leather. This may compensate for the relatively high price of leather. However, good tools make for more fun and effective work, so it is recommended to pay attention to quality tools.

The Workplace

One of the advantages of working with leather is the fact that only a simple workplace is needed. One or two sturdy tables are required. If the tables are covered with plywood, you can hammer or cut without worrying about the surface of the table.

You should always have a stack of newspapers handy to cover the table while gluing, dyeing, or spraying leather. You also need quite a quantity of brown paper for making the cut patterns, preferably an entire roll of packing paper.

Simple boxes are handy for storing tools, rivets and buckles, leather dyes and all other materials. You also need good light, preferably daylight.

Awl

There are several different shapes of awls with various diameters–straight or curved, angular or round. The awl is used to perforate holes in leather to facilitate the hand sewing. Awls are offered with fixed handles, however, an awl grip can be fixed with different kinds of awls and is therefore recommended. The leather to be perforated is best placed on a block of cork. Awls are sold at specialty leather retailers and at building suppliers.

Iron

The ironing of leather is not as frequent as when working with textiles. Nevertheless, it is essential for certain kinds of work, for example when fixing liners. You should never iron on the leather directly, always place an ironing cloth, or even brown paper, between the iron and the leather. A steam iron is not necessary, only a few leathers, like pig velour, are apt for steaming. Leather is best ironed at medium temperatures.

Careful: the embossing of leather is achieved by applying heat and pressure, and it can be damaged by improper ironing.

Before ironing leather, always perform a test on an unobtrusive section.

Snap and rivet machine

Handicraft retailers offer snaps and rivetss which are pressed into the leather, not sewn into it. They are usually sold with the necessary tools and instructions included.

Interfacing

A special interfacing is available for leather (Vliseline LE 420), which is ironed onto the leather at a low temperature. It is thin and soft and can be ironed onto thin leathers, even its entire surface. The leather does not loose its original properties. Vliseline LE 420 is usually sold only at specialized leather shops and retailers.

Fine liner

A fine liner is recommended to mark cut patterns or flawed spots on the reverse side of the leather. A ballpoint pen is probably just as good for this. It is recommended that a test be made to make sure that the color does not bleed through.

Sinew & Thread

Specialty retailers carry leather sinew and thread, which is very tough, but not so much as to tear the perforated holes. Beware of some of the particularly strong threads, as they are intended for industrial-grade machines (or to be sewn by hand) and may destroy the household sewing machine's thread guide. Threads intended for buttons and ornamentation are well suited for sewing robust leathers.

Cutting tools, from left: roll cutter, edge plane, scalpel, knife, scissors

From left: punch, punch forks, punch irons of two sizes, hammer, rubber hammer

Polyester thread of good quality is available in many colors and gauges. If the thread is too thin, it can be doubled. Pure cotton thread is to be avoided, as it can decompose due to the presence of chemicals that are used for tanning leather. To avoid frequent breaking of the thread, it is important to match needle and thread.

Tip: To avoid thread breaking, apply beeswax to the thread prior to sewing. Excess wax is removed by ironing between cloth or rags. You can add a drop of oil onto an entire spool of thread and let it soak into the thread. The thread becomes softer, it does not break anymore, and it is easier to work with. The initial discoloration disappears after the oil has been absorbed. Leather sinews and threads are available at leather retailers.

Rubber mallet

In order to tuck seam allowances or creases, a rubber mallet is necessary. As an alternative, a regular hammer can be covered with leather or textile material. However, be careful not to apply too much force as it can leave pressure marks on the leather. Hammers and rubber mallets can be found at construction retailers and hardware stores.

Glue

It is common to use glue for leather work. A special leather or textile glue is used for gluing seam allowances and creases consistently and with elasticity. A pen for fixing seams replaces stapling and is indispensable for appliqués and the topstitching of bags. These special textile and leather glues do not leave residue on the needle. Use a rubber cement if the glued sections are to be separated again. Leather creases are best glued with "Parva Leather

Line" crease glue for leather. Linings, or leather pieces glued across their entire surface, require an elastic glue. The glue is applied with a brush or palette knife onto the leather and the sections are immediately pressed together. It is important to work quickly here. If the parts that are to be glued together are fairly large, work in sections. Instead of using pins, cut patterns can be fixed onto the leather with an adhesive tape.

All glues are sold at leather specialty stores or well-stocked hobby shops.

Leather grease

Suited for softening and smoothing leather, grease also makes it waterproof and durable. Products based on beeswax are particularly suitable.

Leather knife

Leather or bookbinder knives have a blade that is rounded toward the tip. Specialist workers like to use blades, which can be positioned inside a leather handle. The knife is held like a pen and drawn along a metal ruler for cutting. You should never cut directly on the table, rather, always use a thick padding under the leather. The leather knife is also used to "sharpen" leather, that is, the seam allowances, which are often quite thick, are broken and thinned with an angular cut. Leather knives need to be very sharp and should be sharpened regularly. It is important to always cut in a direction that goes away from the body. Leather knives are sold at specialty leather dealers.

Hollow punches

This tool is available in several different sizes and used for stamping holes and leather circles. In order to avoid

From left: rivet pliers, punch pliers

them becoming blunt too quickly, stamp onto a surface of cardboard or plastic. Hollow punches are available at specialty retailers.

Punch fork

A punch fork consists of three or four tines and is used to perforate the holes for a leather seam. Punch the holes over a base of either cardboard, wood, or plastic to maintain the tines' sharpness. Punch forks are available at construction material retailers, or they can be manufactured from a chisel.

Punch pliers

Punch pliers come with several different sizes of punch diameters. To avoid rapid blunting, place a piece of cardboard below the leather to be punched. Available at specialty retailers.

Wood burning tools

Engravings, patterns, or inscriptions can be done using a wood burning tool on leather. Some retailers offer special adornment wood burning tools that can be used to burn decorative marks.

Needles

The use of the right needles is extremely important when working with leather. A wrong needle, or a faulty needle, will skip stitches or may lead to needle break. Soft leather can be sewn with a regular sewing machine needle, gauge 80; for thicker leather, use gauge 90. For very tough leather there are special leather needles with gauges of 90 to 110, which feature a sharpened, three-sided tip. However, these three-sided needles cut a slit into the leather that can result in tearing, so they should not be used for seams that are under stress, such as the back middle seam of leather pants. The best method to find out a needle's aptitude for a particular leather is trial and error. Manual sewing needles and three-sided needles are available at leather specialty retailers.

Presser foot

In order to avoid the slippage of leather when stitching, a teflon-covered foot or roller foot is used. A big disadvantage of a roller foot is the fact that its structured and chiseled rolls tend to leave marks on the leather. A good alternative is the use of a top transporter, which can be purchased separately for many sewing machines. In order to sew on a zipper, a single presser foot is needed. These articles are available at sewing machine shops and retailers.

Sewing machine

The sewing is done with a special leather sewing machine with top and needle transporters, or with a sturdy home sewing machine (for example, one that features automatic perforation). A few additional items, like special presser feet, make the work easier and yield more beautiful results.

Seaming tape

Seams which require a particular strength should be sewn by including seaming tape. It can be found at specialty retailers.

Adhesive paper tape strips

There are several different areas where adhesive paper tape strips and sections can be used when working with leather.

In order to make a design pattern, an object, such as the bottle on page 150, is covered with tissue paper and then glued over with overlapping paper strips (one layer)—

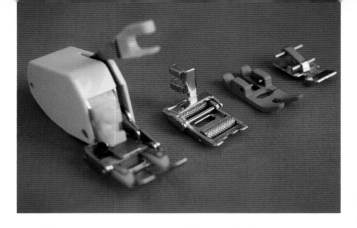

From left to right: top transporter, roll foot, teflon foot, and one-sided zipper foot

the gum-covered side becomes sticky by adding moisture. Once dry, the cardboard-like cover of the object is cut open, providing the design pattern.

Paper strips are also used to stiffen shapes and forms, such as the bowl on page 132. The object is covered with tissue paper and several layers of paper strips until a solid cardboard is achieved. Any shape is possible.

Brown or white paper strips are available at arts and crafts stores.

Punches

Punching or embossing is a technique to engrave relief-like patterns onto leather. Leather derived by vegetal-tanning is best. The punch, an embossing tool, is used to hammer a pattern into the moistened leather (see page 158). Punches can be purchased at leather and specialty handicrafts retailers.

Lacing needle

A lacing needle is necessary in order to guide a leather thread past the hole in the leather in case the thread is not stiff enough by itself. The tip of the thread is held by a spring with small teeth. The thread is not threaded past the needle's eye and therefore it does not bulge. Lacing needles are available through specialty leather shops and handicrafts retailers.

Tailor's chalk

Chalk for garment design is available as a pen, chalk piece, or chalk wheel. The chalk wheel leaves fine lines on the leather. Check whether the chalk can be brushed off before starting. An even better method is to mark the leather on its reverse side with a pen or a fine liner. Tailor's chalk for clothing design is available at handicrafts retailers.

Cutting tools

A sharp roll cutter used with a metal ruler and a cutting base surface makes for perfect leather cuts. Fine cuts can be achieved with a scalpel, with interchangeable blades of different shapes.

A sharp pair of tailor's scissors allows for cutting leather exactly to specification. Tough leather can also be cut with a pair of sharp household scissors. To cut out appliqués, you will need small and pointed scissors.

Tip: To achieve even cuts, do not remove the scissors while cutting and always maintain the same angle.

Transparent adhesive tape

Narrow bands of two-sided self-adhesive tape are suitable for sticking zippers to leather, as they can not be affixed with needles. Creases are also easily fixed with transparent adhesive tape, available at leather and crafts retailers.

Pins

Pins are rarely used when working leather as they leave permanent little holes. If pins are used at all, it is usually with additions to the seam. It is better to use paper clips, photo clips or glue. Some projects are easily fixed with clothespins.

2.2 **Basic Techniques**

Mechanical Surface Treatments

Before there were multiple textiles and leather imitations, the emphasis was on making leather appear less natural and more produced, and on lessening the grain pattern or eliminating it altogether. Leather was lacquered, covered with gold, and embossed, and so it also lost part of its natural characteristics. Nowadays, leather is supposed to emphasize the natural grain patterns and characteristics of leather that set it apart from its imitations.

Leather gets is softness by pulling and stretching the moistened leather by hand, thereby separating the individual fibers. Pommeling is the term used for mechanical softening, particularly of vegetal-tanned fine leather like saffian (morocco). Graining is a process whereby the natural characteristics of the grain patterns are intensified. The slightly moistened leather is rolled over its own edge, with the grain sides facing each other. The resulting fold is then rolled by hand, with a slight pressure across the entire leather surface, until its grain pattern intensifies. When graining leather, a graining wood (see photo) adds to the effect of bringing out the grain structure. Depending on the pressure applied to it, smaller or larger graining patterns emerge, and when working in two directions, the result is a checkered grain pattern.

Pommeling and graining has the effect that the grain shows its natural granulation. Another method uses a wood, shaped like slippers, to roll both fleshy sides of the leather together, providing softness but without emphasizing the grain pattern.

Smooth and brilliant surfaces are achieved by glaze finishing. Rolling a glass roll across the surface while applying

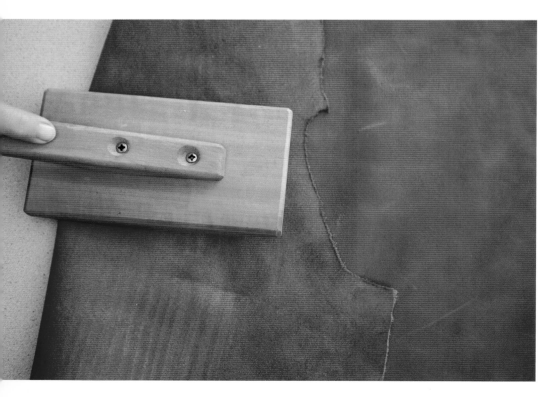

Graining wood

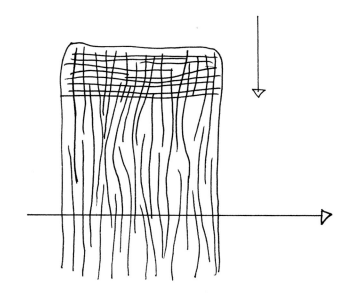

The arrows indicate
the graining direction

pressure results in the leather becoming shiny. This effect is further enhanced when applying a coat of brilliant finish before the process. Another method for achieving lasting brilliance of leather is to iron it with a warm (not hot) iron. Its surface needs to be devoid of dirt and scratches. Matt and velvet-like surfaces result from buffeting the grain side with extremely fine sanding or polishing paper. Sanding the fleshy side long enough will produce a velvety and even surface finish.

Hardening Leather

Back in the Middle Ages, people had already tried to harden leather. Leather armor and containers required very hard and tough leather. There are several methods used to harden leather. Only vegetal-tanned leather can be used, no chrome- or fat-tanned leather. The same basic rule applies here, test the hardening of leather on a scrap piece first.

1   **The Water Method:** This process consists of leaving the leather in hot water for an hour or two, no more than 140 degrees Fahrenheit (60 degrees Celsius). If the water is hotter than that, the leather will shrink. Leave it to dry at a cool and dry location. Leather will darken with this method, but it does not degrade in any way.

2   **The Oven Method:** This method is particularly good for shaping leather into form. Soak the leather briefly in hot water. Pre-heat the oven to between 120 and 200 degrees Fahrenheit (50-100 degrees Celsius). Pull the leather into its desired form and affix it. Place the leather into the turned-off oven until it is dry. Due to the heat, the leather fibers unify into a three-dimensional structure.

3   **The Oven-Wax Method:** If there is the need for truly hard and water-resistant leather and staining or change of color of the surface is not an issue, then this method is quite suitable. The leather is "baked" at about 210 degrees Fahrenheit (100 degrees Celsius) for about half an hour. Meanwhile, heat up beeswax or a candle in a double boiler until it melts. Once the leather is hot through and through, take it from the oven and paint the fleshy side with the hot wax. Repeat this until the leather can no longer absorb wax and has become cold. The wax is absorbed into the grain side and leaves a mottled, dark surface. This method results in the highest fat content of leather.

4   **Hammering** moistened leather also compresses and hardens the cell structure. Use a solid rubber hammer for this method.

5   A much more gentle method for hardening leather is to **coat it** with an ironed-on piece of vliseline/interfacing. Also, a second layer of leather can be glued onto the fleshy side over its entire surface. Both the glue and the second layer of leather provide stiffness, while the leather gets a lining during the process as well. Apply flexible leather glue evenly to both leather parts and then press them together firmly. Use a folding stick to eliminate possible bubbles or creases. Put some heavy books on top of the leather and leave to dry overnight.

Marking and Cutting

The following steps are used when cutting leather:

1   Mark leather flaws and damages, thin patches or holes on its reverse side. Place design patterns outside of these markings.

2   Place the complete design pattern onto the leather. By complete, I mean that you include the parts that lie inside the folds as well as pieces that occur twice, such as the sleeves, which get their own design pattern. When laying out the leather, keep in mind that it stretches less longitudinally than it does laterally. This means that all parts need to face the same direction. You should never cut one piece laterally and the other longitudinally just to save space and leather.

3   Velour leather, just like velvet, has a stroke direction. When it is cut with the stroke direction, it tends to be lighter; when cut against the stroke, it is darker.

The direction you choose is a personal matter, however, both symmetrical pieces should face in the same direction.

4   Fix the design pattern to the back side of the leather using paper tape and draw their outline with a pen or pencil. Add 0.5 to 1 cm to the seams, and 2-3 cm to the edges. Exactly marked seam and edge allowances facilitate putting it together. Sewing lines and other lines or markings are best done by placing carbon paper with the color side down between leather and design pattern and retracing with a copying wheel.

5   Use sharp scissors or a roll cutter to cut the pieces.

Thinning of Edges

This describes the slanted cutting of the leather edges. If the seams of two layers of leather bulge too much, they need to be thinned before they are sewn or glued together. This is not an easy process and it should be done in several passes, with thin layers rather than one thick layer, because it is all too easy to cut through the entire leather.

For thinning the seams, place the leather with the fleshy side up onto a cardboard or wood surface, then cut away leather slivers with a flat-lying knife (always away from the body).

Rivets and Eyelets

In order to unite or strengthen leather pieces, or to affix hollow rivets, you need the right tools. Specialists have tools that avoid the scratching and denting of a rivet. You may be able to find smaller tools with which to hammer in the rivets. Commercially available rivets consist of two parts, the upper and the lower rivet.

Using Rivets
1   Mark the spot to be riveted.
2   Use punch pliers or a punch iron to make a hole in the leather, which should have the thickness of the rivet shaft. If you have large pieces where a rivet needs to be placed in the middle, use a drill.
3   Place the two rivet parts into each other and hammer them together on a sturdy metal surface. To avoid scratches, hammer in the rivets from the back. Do not place leather under it.

Using Eyelets
1   Perforate the leather at its marked spot with the punch pliers. The hole should be a little smaller than the eyelet socket so that it needs to press the leather apart.
2   The eyelet is placed into the hole from the top and reinforced on the back with a ring and placed onto the eyelet tool.
3   Fold over the eyelet with a hammer.

a   edge planer
b   knife

Fasteners and Closures

Zipper

Many projects in this book are sewn with a zipper. The cushions are fitted with a hidden zipper on the back, while the bags, vests, and the leather jacket get zippers where both leather edges meet at the zipper's teeth. This can be a nice effect with zippers of a contrasting color.

Hidden Zipper

For a zipper hidden from both sides, close the seam far enough so as to show only the opening for the zipper. If necessary, glue the seam allowance over to the reverse side of the leather. Carefully hold the closed zipper in place with scotch tape or elastic, and apply liquid glue into the opening, working with the grain side up. Start at the left side of the zipper and sew with the one-sided presser foot about 0.5 cm next to the zipper, from top to bottom. Set a point at the lower edge and continue sewing on the right side of the zipper.

Visible Zipper

A visible zipper is inserted so as to show both leather edges lining up with the zipper teeth. The teeth are therefore visible when the zipper is closed. This method is used for bags and jackets.

To avoid sewing bumps around the zipper, open the zipper about two inches, sew the zipper down to its union; then, while keeping the needle lowered and the presser foot lifted, close the zipper again and continue sewing. Repeat this for the other side.

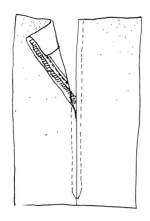 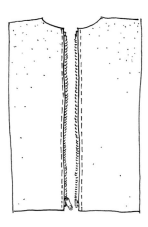

Hidden zipper (both sides)   Visible zipper

Leather Buttons

Leather-covered buttons are more than just a handy solution when no color-matching buttons are available, they are true adornments. Simple round buttons without a bridge are suitable, and only very thin and flexible leather types like lamb nappa, goat split velour or pig velour are usable. If the leather is too thick, it needs to be thinned.

To cover buttons:

1. Cut a leather circle that is slightly larger than the button.
2. Pre-drill the sewing holes with an awl if necessary.
3. Sew in small holes with a strong thread along the edge of the leather. Do not cut off the rest of the thread.
4. Place the button on the center of the back side of the leather and pull the thread tight, causing the leather to stretch tightly around the rim of the button. Use the rest of the thread to sew together the button cross-wise.
5. Use a second piece of leather and cut it to a circle which is slightly smaller than the button and glue it onto the back side of the button. Use a few stitches to affix it.

The entire process is a lot faster if you purchase a complete set at the store. It contains the button form, the design patterns and the necessary tools, together with detailed instructions.

How to make roll or toggle buttons:

1. Cut a triangle of about 7.5 cm length by 2.5 cm width at its baseline.
2. Just before the pointed end, make two holes with an awl, centered, and one below the other.
3. Roll up the leather from its narrow baseline.
4. Mark two slits according to the drawing. These are used to pull the tip of the triangle through them.
5. Cut the marked slits and put glue on the surface, except for the tip.
6. Carefully roll the leather together and pull the tip through the slits.
7. Sew on the roll button through its prepared holes.

Sewing on buttons:

Buttons are always sewn with a little counter button, located on the inside of the leather. There is a distinction between two types: the bridge-type buttons, with a small bridge and a metal eyelet on the lower side, and the button for sewing through, with two or four holes. If they are not used solely for adornment, these buttons are always sewn in with a stem which keeps the two layers of leather from pressing together when the button is closed.

Method

1. Place the closing edges on top of each other so that the edge with the button holes lies on top of the fly guard.
2. Use a pencil to make a perpendicular mark through the top button hole onto the fly guard. This is the spot where the button is sewn on.
3. Buttons should be sewn with doubled thread or special button hole thread. The length of the stem depends on the thickness of the material.
4. Use a match between the holes of the buttons, which is sewn together to provide the distance. Once the stem is wrapped, the match is removed.

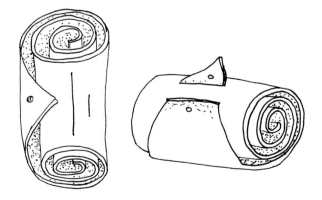

Making toggle buttons

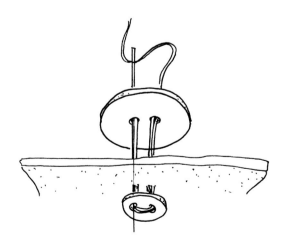

Sewing buttons

Button holes

Real piped button holes are made with two strips in fabrics, but they are not suitable for thick types of leather, because the multiple layers bulge too much. Also, there is no way to affix markings on the top leather surface, and the perforations would adversely affect it. Therefore the following method for making button holes is recommended:

1   Use two leather strips per button hole; cut out four times its width and add 3 cm to the finished pipe.
2   Mark the button hole on both sides.
3   Fold both leather strips lengthwise, the back side inwards, and affix with glue.
4   Glue the leather strips onto the back side of the leather according to the drawing, so that the edges of the strips butt against the button hole marking.
5   Sew narrowly around the button hole from the top side of the leather and cut back the trimming on the back, within the sewing lines, as much as possible.

Stitched button holes are quick and easy to sew. If the leather is too thin, you can iron vliseline/interfacing onto the back of the leather (if there are lines of button holes, use one single piece for all of them), and sew on a facing side. Use a fine liner to mark the button holes. The distance between the button hole line and the finished edge should be three quarters up to the full diameter of the button. Sew around the button hole markings and cut between the stitch lines.

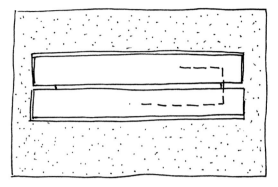

Back side of button hole with facing

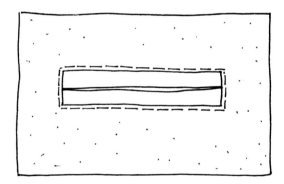

Front side of the finished button hole with facing

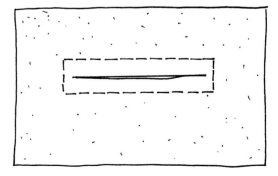

Button hole, simple topstitch

Button loops

Button loops can replace button holes, however, they should match the object's style.

Manufacturing

Design: Since the loops are attached at the edge, a slight change to the design pattern is necessary. The side to which the buttons go can be cut according to the design. On the other side, where the loops are to be placed, mark the center line or finished edge line, add 1.5 cm and you get the new design line. Shorten the trimming if necessary.

Loops: In the case of extremely thin leather, like goat split velour, the loops can be sewn as a sleeve. You will need a leather strip 2-3 cm wide and of the required length. Fold it with the top side inwards. Sew about 0.5 cm from to the edge and trim the seam allowance. Affix a thread with a heavy-gauge leather needle to one end. Knot the thread tightly to the needle and push the needle with its eye first through the leather strip until the strip turns.

Heavier leathers are to be folded with the top side outwards and lengthwise, then sew next to the edge. Trim the seam allowance.

Sewing: Before dividing the leather strip into individual loops, place a loop onto the edge (1). The size of the loops depends on the buttons used. The formula is half the button circumference plus seam allowance. Then, cut all loops.

Glue the loops top side against top side onto the edge and affix with an additional glue strip (2). Glue the trimming top side against top side over the loops and stitch onto the closing edge (3). Trim the seam allowances and turn the trimming inside out. When finished, narrowly stitch the edge (4).

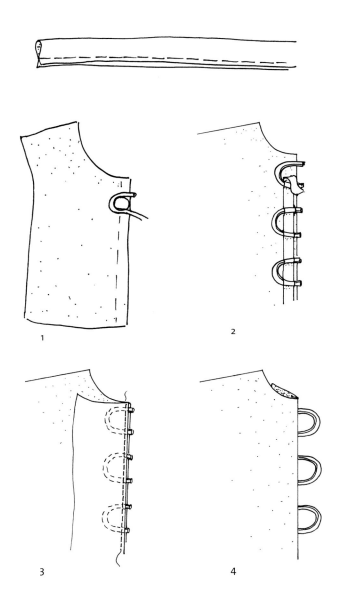

Finishing Leather Edges

For edges rounded towards the outside (1), cut out the seam allowance at short intervals to the seam line in V-shape. The seam allowance can now be pushed together without wrinkling.

For edges rounded towards the inside (2), cut the seam allowance towards the seam line. Once the edge is tensioned it should form a straight line. The seam allowance can stretch now.

A slight rounding usually only requires shortening of the seam allowance.

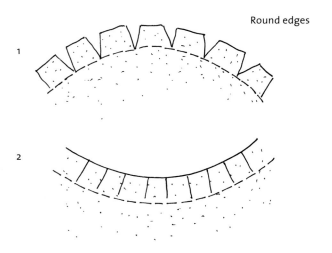

Round edges

Leather Seaming

Leather can be seamed, although it does not have to, as its edges do not fray. To fix leather seams, do not use pins but instead, use paperclips, flexible glue in tubes, or double-sided adhesive tape.

The seam line is marked and the seam allowance is trimmed to 2 cm. If the leather is rather heavy, the edges need to be thinned. Put glue on the seam allowance or affix with two-sided tape. Fold the seam and flatten it. Then affix the seam from the back side with slight hammer strokes.

Sew the seam with long stitches on the top side according to your needs. Using a ruler results in nice and straight seam lines

Basics of Leather Sewing Techniques

Once sewn, leather seams can not be opened again, as the puncture holes will always remain visible; therefore, it is advisable to precisely mark the seam lines on the leather. Staples and pins should not be used at all, as the parts can be accurately affixed with paperclips or with elastic leather glue.

Machine Sewing

Despite the numerous types and makers of sewing machines, all of them pretty much follow the same design. They are all suitable for sewing thin leather. Consumer sewing machines without a top transporter often cause the leather to become stuck at the presser foot (see page 54). If you do not have a teflon presser foot you can put talcum or chalk powder, even starch flour, onto the seams. Try out this method on a piece of scrap leather to see if it can be easily removed.

Leather is not sewn with back stitches, but by leaving a 10 cm piece of thread and knotting the thread ends at the back with a half hitch knot. When sewing over thick seams, the sewing machine may skip for a few stitches. To avoid this, place a folded piece of leather or fabric under the presser foot so that the presser foot remains on the same level.

Seam allowances need to be stroked apart with the fingers or with a cold iron and are then either glued or topstitched together.

The right balance between needle and thread is crucial for a clean seam. It the needle is too thin for the particular leather type, it will skip often. The length of the stitch should be fairly large for leather, as it tends to tear due to its structure. A longer stitch leaves fewer holes and perforates less. Before starting work, make sure that you test the needle, thread, and length of stitch, and adjust if necessary.

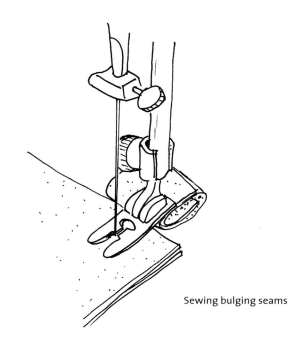

Sewing bulging seams

Here is a table for basic orientation:

Leather	Thread	Needle	Stitch length
thin: goat, sheep, fat-tanned leather	polyester	leather needle (angular tip) gauge 75/90	2–3 mm (8-10 stitches per inch)
medium: nappa, calf	polyester	leather needle (angular tip) gauge 90	2–3 mm (8-10 stitches per inch)
thick: cow, horse, box calf	polyester, gauge 50-70	leather needle (angular tip) gauge 90/110	2,5–4 mm (6-10 stitches per inch)

Tip: Before starting out, make sure that there is sufficient lower thread on the spool.

Thin leather can be sewn like fabric, that is, stitching top side to top side, spread seam allowances, and stitch or glue in place. The edges can be turned over and sewn together.

Thick leather is sewn with an open topstitch. Cut the design with one side including seam allowance, the other without it. On the back side of the side without allowance, mark the allowance of the other side and affix with a fixing pen. Glue the seam allowance of the side with seam allowance with its top side onto the previously marked seam. Topstitch the seam from the top side.

Hand Sewing

Compared to other fixing methods like glue and rivets, seams have the advantage of being flexible, staying flexible, and not being weakened by moisture. Saddler thread made from hemp or linen is used to sew leather pieces together, and it needs to be strong enough not to tear when the stitches are tightened. Special leather thread is pre-waxed to prevent thread tear and knotting while sewing. Unwaxed thread should be treated with beeswax or paraffin from a candle. If you place the thread between two paper tissues and iron it, the wax will permeate to the center of the thread.

The tighter you pull the thread, the lower the slack between pieces and, hence, the less shearing effect is present. The distance between stitches needs to be large enough so that the leather will not be perforated nor tear apart. The distance from the seam to the edge needs to be even and it is marked prior to sewing using a ruler. For the seam length to remain even, markers are placed at even intervals on the seam line. There are several methods:

- Use a perforating fork for hammering in evenly spaced slits.
- Use a special copying wheel and run it along the seam. These wheels are available with different dis-

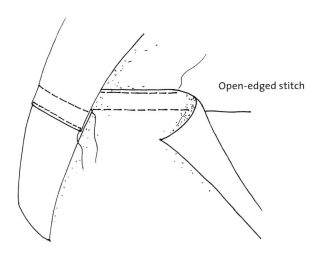

Open-edged stitch

Making holes with a punch fork

tances between markers and can be purchased at specialty handicrafts and leather retailers.

– Use a template to mark the stitches and pre-drill them with an awl. For thin leather threads, use the punch pliers or the punch iron. Choose about 3 mm as a distance for sewing with thread and about 5-6 mm for sewing with leather threads.
– Another method is to run the sewing machine without thread and with a high stitch length to perforate the leather, then use the resulting holes for hand sewing.

It is not advisable to regularly knot or safeguard the thread. The thread should be cut to the length of your outstretched arms, which is the optimal thread length.

Tip: Do a test run of different seams on a scrap piece, this saves you a lot of calculations.

The following are the basic hand stitches:

Saddle Stitch

This is the most common hand stitch for sewing leather. Its appearance most resembles that of a machine stitch. First, pre-drill the holes with an awl. Double the thread and place a needle on each end. Sewing is done with both needles at the same time by pulling up the end of the thread with one needle and pushing down the other thread with the other needle.

Both threads always meet at one hole. Pull through one thread fully before sewing the other one. Pull both threads tight.

Whip Stitch

Leather edges are decorated with a simple whip stitch. This stitch does not tolerate much tension and it does not replace a seam. The effect of a drawstring can be achieved by slightly moistening the leather, placing the edges on top of each other, and pulling the thread really tight.

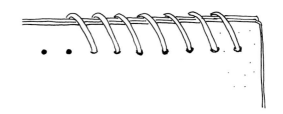

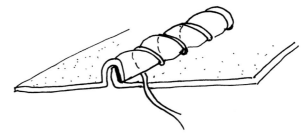

a   Saddle stitch
b   Whip stitch
c   Drawstring-effect
    with whip stitch

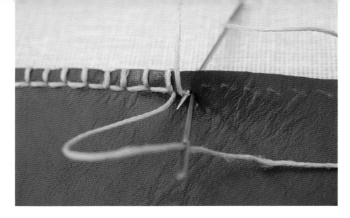

Moccasin stitch

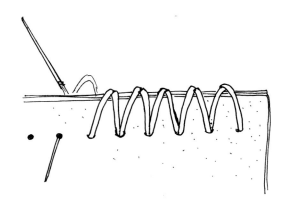

Cross or cruiser-stitch

Moccasin Stitch

The moccasin stitch holds the edges together and reinforces them nicely. It is used on soft leather like moccasin leather. For every stitch to appear like a square, the length of the stitch and the distance to the edge must be equal. Pre-drill the holes with an awl. Use two needles to sew. The stitch is composed of a combination of the whip stitch and the saddle stitch.

Thread one needle at each end of the thread. Place thread over the edge and thread through the first hole from both sides. Sew a saddler stitch with both needles. Then, take one of the needles over the edge and once again through the same hole. After this, another saddle stitch and, again, take one of the threads across the edge. The whip stitch is always done from the same side, no matter left or right. As the needles change side at each stitch, the thread ends alternate when lying across the edge. So the thread lengths remain the same. Lock the seam with two to three back stitches.

Cruiser Stitch

This stitch is used to strengthen edges while decorating them as well. It is not quite as tear-resistant as the moccasin stitch since it is missing the topstitch, and hence it should only be used for seams that will not be overly abused. The stitches should be of the same length as the distance to the edge, just like the moccasin stitch.

The cruiser stitch consists of two whip stitches. It is performed with two needles. The difference from the simple whip stitch is the fact that the needles cross the edge at each stitch before being threaded into the next hole. The needles need to always be crossed in the same fashion so that the threads lie across the edge evenly. Lock the seam by stitching back a few steps.

Mattress Stitch

This is a special upholstery stitch used for invisibly sewing together two leather or cloth sections at their edges. A curved, sharp needle is used to close the last remaining open seams—for example, after upholstering—so the seam is invisible.

Turn the seam allowance of the seam to be closed over to the inside. Make a safety knot at the end of the thread. First, the needle stitches one inner edge in and out. Slightly offset, the other inner edge is stitched in as well as out. After two or three stitches, place the edges on top of each other and tighten the thread quite a bit. Because of the offset stitches, the thread pretty much disappears. Lock the end of the seam with a few back stitches.

Adornment Stitch

The adornment stitch is used for uniting folded edges with a flat surface, for adding pockets, or for sewing appliqués and jacket linings.

Sewing is done right to left. Lock the thread and sew the needle and the thread into the edge. Exactly above the exit point, sew into the opposite leather or fabric side, make a small stitch and sew again vertically at the opposite side into the edge. Sew out after 0.5 mm. Tighten the thread only lightly between the stitch edges.

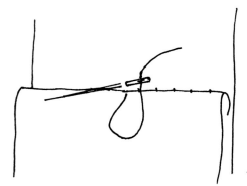

Adornment stitch

Sewing with leather threads or strings

Thread wears out faster than leather. If seams are exposed to a lot of friction, it is best to use a rawhide string rather than thread. There are leather threads made from a specially treated and very hard leather which is usually sold in bands of 3, 4, or 5 mm width and a thickness of 1 mm. These can be worked while dry or moist. While dry, rawhide string is very hard and not easily manipulated. But slightly moistened, it becomes flexible and soft. To moisten it, place the string briefly into hot water and leave it inside a dry cloth. This way the moisture gets absorbed. If the seams are very long, wrap the string into a moist cloth again. If the string is too wet, it will stretch and become longer while sewing.

Leather strings can be purchased in several lengths, colors, and gauges, either as suede or as smooth leather, usually at leather retailers. However, leather bands and strings can be cut out in a spiral by anyone. Usually a piece of about 1 meter is enough for sewing. The commercially available leather strings are stiff enough that they do not require a string needle. Softer strings can be sharpened at the end and then coated with glue. Once dry, the leather is stiff at the tip and does not require a needle at all.

Basically, all of the stitches which can be performed with thread can also be done with leather strings. However, there are certain seams which gain a lot with the use of a leather thread, for example, decorative edging with leather thread. A beautiful and decorative stitch requires that the leather thread not be twisted. It has to lie flat with the grain side up, either on the edge or on the grain side.

It is quite complicated to lock the thread at the end of the stitch when using leather strings. Back stitches are very visible and not recommended. A simple but not very pleasing method is to knot the thread on the back side. The knot should be flattened with a hammer. The best method for locking beginning and/or end of the thread is to place the leather thread into the seam and clasp it tight by tightening the stitches. The end of the thread can also be fixed with a little glue.

Whip Stitch

The easiest connection is to stitch the edges with a whip stitch (see page 67). Place the end of the leather thread between the two leather pieces. The edge is sewn together from hole to hole, always tightening the thread between stitches. Once you get to the end of the leather string, cut it off except for 1 cm and sharpen its end. Take the new thread, also sharpened at the tip, and place it into the following hole and glue both ends together. Once dry, tighten the new thread or string and continue sewing. When done, the tip and end are again united by gluing them together. Use a rubber mallet to flatten the seam.

One very decorative method to adorn leather edges is to use a whip stitch with three leather bands, threads, or strings.

For it to appear neat and jewelry-like, the correct relation between the thread's thickness, the distance to the edge, and the distance between holes is essential. For example, a good-looking seam uses a leather string of 3 mm width, an edge distance of 5 mm, and a hole distance of 6 mm. It is best to practice on a scrap piece first.

First, mark the stitches and pre-drill them with the awl. Work from right to left. Thread the first string from the back to the front past the first hole, take it across the edge and thread it from the back past the fourth hole. Tighten the thread. Pull the second string through the second hole (always work from the back to the front), take it across the edge and thread it past the fifth hole from the back. Do the same with the third string at the third and the sixth hole.

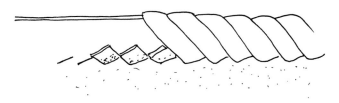

Whip stitch with three leather strips

Blanket or Vienna stitch

Repeat the procedure by threading the first string past the seventh and tenth hole, the second string past the eighth and eleventh hole, and the third string past the ninth and twelfth hole. No open spaces are made because the strings lie exactly next to each other due to their inclination. To lock the ends, punch though one single layer of leather and anchor between the stitches.

Saddle Stitch

The saddle stitch can also be done with leather threads or strings (see page 67). Because of the thicker gauge of the leather threads, it is necessary to widen the hole with an awl.

Blanket or Vienna Stitch

This decorative stitch is used for sewing leather edges. Pre-drill the holes with an awl. It is best to work right to left, with the needle and the leather edge pointing towards you.

Leave a short section at the end for securing it later. Start by taking the leather string from the front to the back past the first hole and immediately thread into the next left-handed hole, also from front to back. Before passing the needle through the third hole, pass the thread from front to back past the previous stitch and then, again, stitch from the front to the back past the following pre-drilled hole. Pull the thread tight, the resulting braid should be running across the edge.

You need to experiment as to how tight the thread needs to be pulled. When sewing peripherally, the tip and the end of the thread meet. Either you knot the thread where it is not visible, or glue the ends together after sharpening them.

The blanket stitch can be used for trimming, or to unite two pieces of leather. The latter leaves the impression of the stitch being braided.

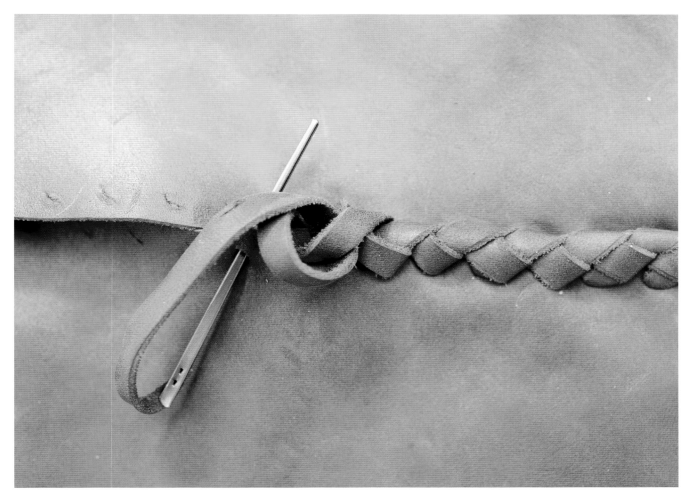

Uniting two pieces of leather with the blanket or Vienna stitch

Buttonhole Stitch

The buttonhole stitch is not only useful for trimming button holes but can also be applied for decorating borders and edges. Use a scrap piece to test the distance between holes that you need. The drawing shows how the thread passes through the holes and loops. It is best to hold the loops between the thumb and index finger of the left hand. This assures that the leather thread is always lying nicely. As before, you need to experiment with the tightness of the thread.

The buttonhole stitch appears quite bulgy when done with a leather string. Pre-drill the holes with an awl. Leave an extra piece of thread at the start for later finishing or locking. Place the thread around the tip of the needle, then pull the needle through and tighten the thread. The resulting knot should lie on top of the edge.

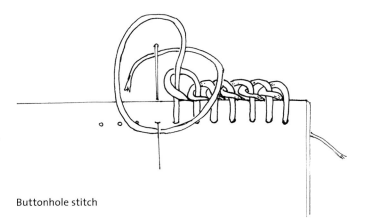

Buttonhole stitch

3

Leather Garments

3.1 The Origin of Clothing

The history of clothing is as old as human culture. As leather was one of the first materials from which clothing was made, it plays a particular role. The oldest clothes were most likely made from the hides of hunted animals. This natural resource was then cleaned and turned into pants, skirts and coats.

The question is, why do humans put on a second skin, contrary to all other living beings. The usual explanation is that people wanted to protect themselves from wind and rain with clothing. This is certainly true, however, this explanation as to the origin of clothing is rather unlikely, as our first skin had been sufficient before inventing clothing, and it still is today (in many temperate climate zones).

The following needs may have contributed to the origin of clothing:

1   **Clothes as protection:** The more humans descended from their ancestors, the animals, the more they lost their natural "protective garment." It is not clear whether the loss of our own hair led to the manufacturing of clothes, or whether the wearing of foreign skins led to the loss of our hair.

2   **Animal skin as a hunting strategy:** The earliest proof of a second skin can be seen on cave paintings from about 15,000 to 10,000 BC. The image shows a human dressed in a deer hide. The semi-erect walk, as well as his hands and feet, show that it is a hunter dressed in a deer hide. This allows him to get close to deer that are to be hunted. The antler is an indication that this is not for protection against climate conditions. The hunter not only slips into the hide, he also enters the spirit of the animal and gains power. This leads to shamanism, which is still practiced in many parts of the world, as well as to magic proceedings and dances while dressed in animal costumes.

3   **Cultural skin to hide the sexual organs:** The body does not need a second skin in warm climates, however, loincloths and aprons are often worn, usually in connection with cultural rules and rituals. The sense of shame is certainly a function of clothing and not an original function, as humans could only have developed a sense of shame after hiding certain body parts in the first place.

4   **Clothing as adornment:** The urge to decorate and adorn oneself must be as old as humanity itself. Man has always done a lot more regarding his clothing than what was strictly necessary to protect against heat and cold. He continuously designed new forms and shapes and adorned the clothes with color and patterns. Some researchers speculate that clothing developed out of jewelry. As proof, they point to the fact that there are no natural peoples who are not adorned, though there are those who have no clothing. It can be assumed that a nice hide or skin has always been more than just a practical item.

Garments and clothing as such started their enormous growth in the development of textile techniques with fine, flexible thread material. The natural second skin, the animal skin, was preferred in cold climate zones, particularly by hunters and horsemen, over artificial or textile material, for the following two reasons:

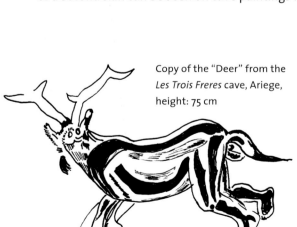

Copy of the "Deer" from the *Les Trois Freres* cave, Ariege, height: 75 cm

1   Leather is organic and adjusts better to the shape of the body than geometric textile surfaces.
2   Leather can be cut with a knife, resulting in a clean cutting surface, whereas textile cloth could only be cut with the later development of scissors, and the fraying cutting edges needed to be finished.

Whereas leather has always been the most common material for shoes, it has only been re-incorporated for daily use during the last thirty years. Around 1920, leather was used primarily for pilot or motorcycle jackets and caps, as well as pants. These garments had the notions of adventure and manliness attached to them. While some women took advantage of this image, they remained an exception. These associations fit well into the general image of the rebellious youth movements and cultures of the 20th century—for example, rockers and punks—who wore their protest on their skin, figuratively and literally. The fetish scene still considers black, shiny leather to be attractive, which is why leather has this slightly morbid image.

The leather industry and fashion takes these different images into consideration and produces leather for every personality type, and leather is well established for everyday clothing nowadays. Coats, jackets, dresses, shirts, T-shirts, vests, sports clothing, pants, and skirts are made form leather, which has proven to be not only very robust and long-lived, but also smooth and soft for wearing. Clothing made from leather is breathable, it absorbs humidity and allows it to vaporize—leather "breathes." Millions of fine air pockets between the cells provide warmth in winter as well as coolness in summer. Leather is therefore an ideal material for garments and clothing.

One very important factor for making a purchase decision is the "grip" of leather. The look, smell, and grip allow for a direct feel of the leather and a mental image of the garment to be made. When you get close to the touch of leather, as is the case with garments made from leather, specific gender-related issues and imaginations come into play. For example, goat and cow leather is considered more "male" than i.e. lamb leather, which is more "female" as to its associated image.

Soft leathers are used for loose fashion, elegance is achieved with smooth leathers, and matt, firm, as well as elastic leathers with strong grains look sportive.

Garments which are worn close to the body are often made from New Zealand lamb velour or lamb nappa. Its velvety surface, its numerous color variations, and its soft and flowing texture allow for it to be made into shirts, dresses, jackets, or vests. Lamb leathers can be sewn with regular household sewing machines with the right presser foot, just like cloth fabrics.

Firm, heavy and thick cow hides are used for protective clothing like motorcycle jackets or pilot jackets, and for leather pants as well.

The Design Pattern

Leather allows one to sew pretty much any kind of garment. Ready-made design patterns can be purchased commercially. Usually, the packages indicate the level of difficulty for making a particular garment, as well as information about the necessary implements like zippers and the amount of fabric (see page 46 for calculating it for leather). The package contains detailed sewing instructions with text and images. All design patterns which are not used for elastic fabrics, like common cotton fabrics, jeans, and heavy wool fabrics, can be applied for leather manufacturing. Designs which are a little wider and not too close to the body are suitable. Choose the same size you would choose for a garment made from cloth.

The most common design patterns are intended for bulk fabrics and they are not always the best choice for leather, which is measured in square feet. Also, their irregular shape and the relatively small hides from goats and sheep make the layout of the design patterns rather challenging. One basic rule dictates that you need some 30 square feet for a short jacket and about 60 square feet for a three-quarter jacket. A vest requires about two hides; for a jacket with sleeves, add about two more hides, depending on the width of the sleeves. In order to not miscalculate the required leather, take the design patterns to the leather dealer and lay them out on the leather pieces.

Trimming and edging are not necessary for leather working. This should be edited on the design pattern beforehand. If the individual design pattern pieces are too large for the skins, it is necessary to include the characteristic dividing seams. Depending on the design, they can be worked into the garment with much effect.

Size: Ready-to-use patterns are offered as sets of several sizes. In order to figure out the correct pattern size you need to take your own measurements first. The relevant tables for calculation are printed on the pattern. Do not wear thick clothing and do not use an elastic tape line when taking measure.

Breast circumference	measured below the arms and across the widest part of the back and the most voluminous part of the breast.
Waist circumference	this is the narrowest part of the waist.
Hip circumference	measured at the widest part of the hip, about 20-25 cm below the waist.
Side length	measured at the side from the waist to the ground.

Take note of the following: Leather has neither warp nor weft—hence there is no run of thread—although it does have a tear direction (see page 46). Leather does stretch, though it does not shrink.

Based on your own measures, the size of the design pattern is determined.

Transferring the Paper Patterns

Once the correct design pattern size has been determined, the patterns are transferred onto tissue or brown paper. Tissue paper is placed on top of the design and the seam lines are copied by tracing them. Place brown paper below the design pattern and run a tracing wheel along the pattern. The teeth of the wheel leave a thin perforated line on the paper. Cut out the design sections.

The design patterns need to be modified for leather garments. Those that lie within the fold should be cut out as complete or double sections. This is best done first on brown paper. Each part gets its own pattern. Those sections which are to be cut twice like the front left and right side, or the sleeves, should be copied and marked Left and Right. Keep in mind that a section might be flipped, or you may end up with two parts for one side and none for the other.

All of the markings on the pattern are to be marked on the leather as well. The seam allowance of 0.5 cm to 1 cm at all seams, as well as the 3 to 4 cm at the edges and the length of the sleeves, are added only on the leather. But they need to be considered beforehand.

Before cutting out the leather, take some time and check whether the design really fits nicely. Sew a test piece from a scrap piece of untreated cotton, for example. After fitting, mark off possible changes and transfer them onto the paper design. This is necessary, as leather seams, once unstitched, leave thin puncture holes behind. Once everything fits perfectly, lay out the pattern on the leather.

Tip: Lined garments are best fitted and checked after sewing in the lining.

Before laying out the pattern, check the top leather side for possible damages. Hold up the entire hide or piece of leather against a light source and check for thin patches, holes, or cuts. Mark all irregular spots on the back side with either a soft pencil or a fine-liner. Place the pattern outside of these spots and try to conserve as much surface as possible.

3.4 **The Lining**

Leather keeps its original skin properties, which means that, just like our skin, it changes with time. Through movement and humidity, leather will fit the shape of the body, however, lining materials do not. Woven lining materials should therefore be cut to allow for some extra space for movement, otherwise they may not hold up to the stress and tear. For this reason, lining materials are selected according to their toughness and durability. Check that the care and maintenance properties of the lining match those of the leather. If the leather can be washed, the same should apply for the lining material.

3.5 **Aviator Helmet or Cap** 🟫🟫🟫

Because of its great properties, leather protects particularly well against adverse climate conditions. The aviator helmet is one of the protective caps, working nicely even without an airplane around. This helmet or cap is particularly neat on a bicycle, as both head and ears are covered and the cap does not fly away. Made from soft lamb nappa or calf leather and lined with a soft velour and flannel, this cap keeps you warm in winter and it looks great. Natural brown or creamy white give it a real classic look. The design emulates a 1920s design. It is composed of five design sections.

Material and tools
design pattern (a)
large piece of calf nappa, natural brown
small piece of pig velour, beige
0.30 m of flannel
press-button
thread in matching color
sewing machine
glue
spiritus in spray bottle
hat maker's wooden head, if available

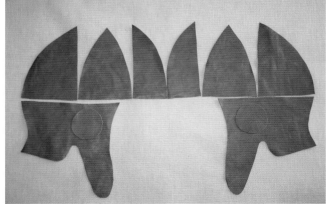

Work stages

1 Enlarge design parts 1 to 5. (a)

2 For the outer cap, place the sections 1 to 5 twice each in the same direction onto the fleshy side of the leather, conserving as much surface as possible. Use a pen to trace the outlines and add 0.5 cm of seam allowance, then cut out.

3 The head segments 1 to 3 need to be sewn together piece by piece, top to top, spread seam allowances and glue them. (b and c)

4 Spray the cap with spiritus and shape it over a hat-maker's head. (d)

5 Topstitch the lining flannel just like the outer cap, piece by piece, place cap inside the other and stitch the circumference, leaving a small hole for turning the cap later.

6 Glue the ear piece (5) onto the lower cap section (4) and topstitch around the outline.

7 Sew together both lower sections of the cap at the middle of the back part.

8 Line the lower cap section with velour (e and f), the upper edge remains open and is placed onto the cap from the inside, center on center. To finish, topstitch around the entire cap with a narrow edge.

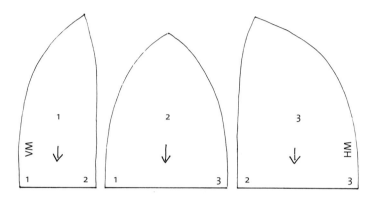

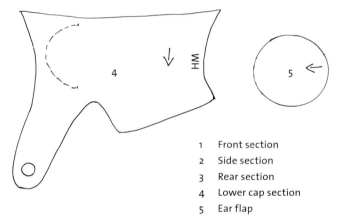

a

1 Front section
2 Side section
3 Rear section
4 Lower cap section
5 Ear flap

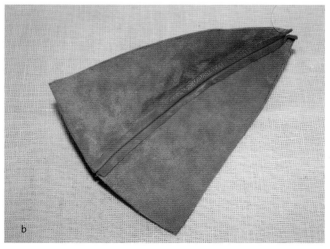

b

c

d

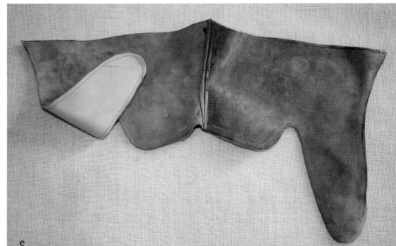

e

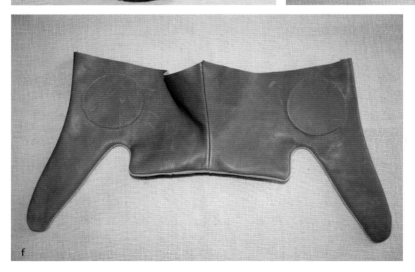

f

3.6 **T-Shirt**

With a t-shirt design pattern, soft goat split velour, a zipper, and a crochet needle you can make yourself a dandy top. The sleeves of the pattern need to be shortened so as to fit onto leather pieces, leaving enough leather scraps for the crochet inserts. Instead of crochet inserts, other adornment techniques such as appliqués, embroidery, painting, or printing can be used. Edge finishing is not necessary. In general, however, the garments maintain their shape better if the outer edges are folded and glued or sewn.

Material and tools
t-shirt design pattern
goat split velour, two skins, about 12 sq. ft (1.12 m²)
sharp scissors
matching thread
two-way zipper, 40 cm (can be opened from the top or the bottom)
leather sewing machine (or sewing machine with teflon presser foot or top transporter)
glue
punch pliers
crochet needle, no. 3.5

Work stages

1   Lay out the design sections on the back sides of the two leathers, always conserving space and in the same direction. Beware: lamb skins have a particularly developed back structure which often differs in coloration, which should be taken into account when laying out the patterns.

2   Mark the sections on the leather. Add 0.5 cm of seam allowance to the seams running longitudinally, as well as to the shoulder seams; mark 1.5 cm of seam allowance to the lower sleeve cuts, the sleeves, the neckline and at the lower edge. Cut out the sections. (a, b and c)

3   Pin together the leather sections, but only within the seam allowances, as pins leave lasting holes in the leather.

4   Topstitch the front dividing seams top side to top side and fold and glue both seam allowances towards the center. Sew a narrow edge from the top side. (d, e and f)

5   Topstitch the side seams top side to top side, put glue onto the back side of the seam allowances and use your finger nails to pull them apart and glue them on.

6   Topstitch the shoulder seams and finish the seam allowances the same as with the side seams.

7   Place the short sleeve as shown in Figure g

8   Before adding the zipper, fold and glue the seam allowances of the center edge of the right and left front section to their back side. Glue the zipper under the edges so that it is visible when finished. Sew the zipper about a presser foot's width from top to bottom, keeping a distance of 0.5 cm from the edge.

9   To finish, pinch the seam allowances at the lower part of the sleeve cut and at the neckline just before the seam line, and fold and glue to the back side. Topstitch the edges and cut back the seam allowances. Only fold and glue the edge allowances at the sleeves and the lower edge.

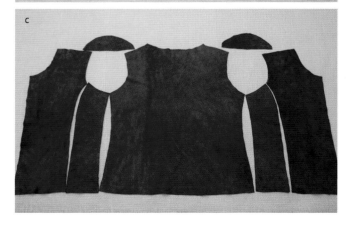

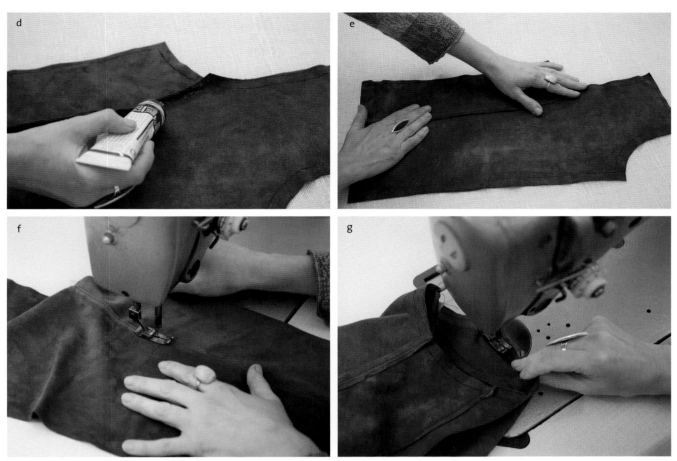

Crochet edges

1 Cut 2-3 mm wide leather strips from scrap leather in a circular fashion and wind them up.

2 Place even marks of 1 cm distances at the lower edge and the sleeve cuts. The distance to the edge needs to be even. Punch small holes into the leather with punch pliers. (h)

3 When starting the first row, crochet three chain stitches. Chain stitches result from pulling the leather thread from the back through the first hole, which results in the first stitch. When three such chain stitches have been done, put the leather thread around the needle and push into the pre-drilled hole and grab leather thread again. Again, grab leather thread and pull it onto the crochet needle past the first two stitches. Place the leather thread around the needle and pull it past the next two stitches onto the needle. Push into the next hole, etc. Repeat stitch order for two rows. (i to o)

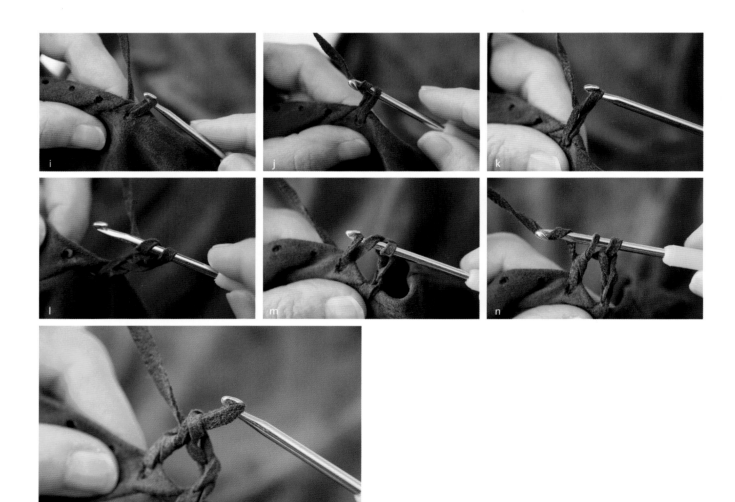

For a leather vest, the best method is to use a jacket design pattern without the sleeves. Almost all jacket patterns are suitable, except those with raglan sleeves.

The particular advantage of working with leather is that, contrary to fabrics, the edges need not be trimmed or neatened. This means that the seam allowances can be placed outwards as part of the individual design characteristics. This underscores the segmented character of the vest or jacket.

The shown vest is without lining and yet it is warm, close to the body, and outlining the body shape. It does not bulk, it fits under every coat, and it can be taken on any trip as your favorite piece. It is also easier to sew than you may think.

Material and tools
design pattern
calf leather
two-way zipper, 60 cm long
matching thread
elastic glue
sewing machine
sharp scissors

Work stages

1   Cut out the design patterns and double them if necessary so that each leather segment has its own pattern. Number the cut sections.

2   Lay out the cut patterns so as to not leave excess leather, paying attention to the direction of the leather. Add 0.5 cm of seam allowance and cut the sections. (a and b)

3   Glue together all sections piece by piece, back side to back side, and sew together. Make sure that the distances to the edges stay about the same.

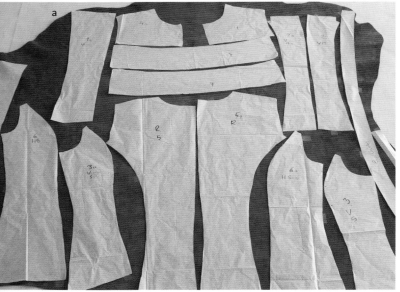

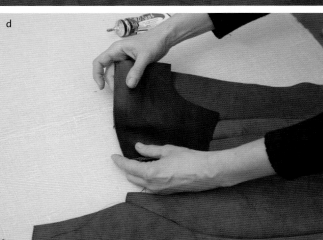

4   Glue the yoke back to back to the front piece and sew it on. (c and d)

5   Close the upper shoulder seams. (e)

6   Sew together both collar sections back to back and sew from the inside to the upper edge of the vest.

7   Finally, sew in the zipper so it remains visible (see page 60).

3.8 Leather Jacket

Basically, this leather jacket is sewn the same way as the vest, as both garments have the same basic design. However, the following items have been changed:

1 The collar of the jacket consists of only one pattern segment, which is laid out twice. This saves one seam, which could be bothersome at the neck and chin.
2 The jacket is slightly longer than the vest.
3 The jacket has sleeves.
4 The jacket is lined.

Material and tools

The same materials and tools are used as for the vest, but this time the sleeves are not left out. A firm lining fabric is added, the size of which is calculated according to the design.

a

b

Work stages

1 It is best to start with the lining of the jacket. The lining is cut according to the same patterns as those for leather, however, the front trimming, sleeve trimming and the collar are subtracted. Add 1-1.5 cm of seam allowance to all edges and cut the sections.
2 Sew the lining according to the pattern and iron it.
3 Since the lining stays loose at the edge of the jacket, iron, fold and sew the edge allowance towards the inside at about 2 cm above the marked edge line.
4 Try on the lining. If any corrections are necessary, they can still be done and transferred to the design pattern.
5 The work stages for the leather jacket are the same as those for the vest, steps 1 to 5 included. Note that the collar is cut from one piece.
6 The collar is glued back to back onto the collar cut so that the lower collar lies at the bottom. The allowances are lying towards the outside. The collar begins and ends at the closing edge.
7 Fold the collar lengthwise in half, back side inside.

8 Glue the zipper in between the collar openings and the edging and top leather so that it is visible, then sew down narrowly.
9 Sew together the sleeve sides back to back and leave a gap of about 10 cm at the top of the sleeve's edge. (a)
10 Glue the sleeve edging back to back onto the sleeve and sew the sleeve edges narrowly.
11 Place the sleeves back to back into the jacket and follow the top sleeve circle so that the sleeve fits exactly into the opening. (b) Sew the seams.
12 Place the lining back to back into the jacket so that the seams touch each other. Fold and pin the edges at the trimmings and the rear neck opening.
13 Use a sharp leather needle to sew the lining with the adornment stitch (see page 68) onto the front trimmings, the sleeve trimmings and the rear collar.
14 Sew the collar seam with the trimming and the lining from the outside. Take care to place the seam right next to the existing seam.

Leather Skirt

This leather skirt is made from a rather matt, almost greasy, chrome-tanned and anilin-dyed calf leather without any top coating. It really wears quite well. The design is easy to make and it does not require any tucks. This is good news, as the tips of the tucks tend to bulge with firm leather.

The best way is to use a simple skirt design, perhaps one which has proven to be right when made from cloth. The retailers for design patterns carry a large selection of patterns for skirts consisting of several panels in their catalogs. If you don't have a suitable skirt design handy, simply divide a basic skirt pattern into eight pieces. Make sure that the dividing seams are located within the tucks, in order that they may flow directly into the seam.

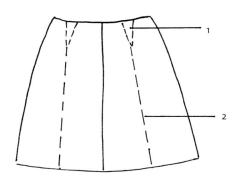

Tuck

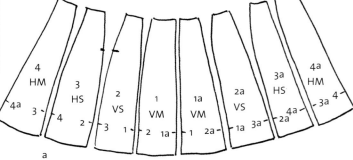

New cut lines

Leather has clean cutting edges, so the seams can be placed outwards as part of the design elements, as with this skirt. It emphasizes the skirt's panels and its striped characteristics. Open edges can be dyed with the color of the leather's surface, or with a contrasting color in case they are not dyed through with anilin dyes.

Material and tools

---

calf skin

---

prepared design pattern (a)

---

firm vliseline/interfacing

---

matching thread

---

zipper (length according to design pattern, about 12 to 20 cm)

---

scissors

---

glue

---

sewing machine

Work stages

1 Divide the design into eight parts, four frontal and four back segments. Double the pattern sections so that each skirt segment gets its own section. Mark the segments. (a) This is important so as not to mix up the sections. (For example: F1L= front section 1 left, B1R=back section 1 right). Mark the length of the zipper on the left side.

2 Place the pattern sections (in a way so as to conserve leather) onto the fleshy or back side of the leather, fix with glue strips and mark outlines. Seam allowance is 0.5 cm at all longitudinal sides, 1 cm at the waist band, and 2 cm at the lower edge. Cut the sections.

3 Place the zipper inside: first, sew the left side segments up until the zipper marker, glue the zipper in place, and sew so that both faces are hidden (see page 60). Then sew the rest of the segments together piece by piece. (b)

4 The waistband gets an extra layer of vliseline/interfacing ironed on (anilin-tanned leather does not withstand much heat, so put the iron on a low heat position). Fold the waistband lengthwise and at its center and trim the top skirt edge. Sew from the top side.

If you want to trim the skirt, simply fold and glue the lower edge some 1.5 cm inwards. There is no need for sewing, and the edge would only get unnecessarily stiff.

b

c

3.10 **Leather Pants**

Leather pants are sewn as indicated on the design pattern. Often the size of the leather hides is not sufficient for a design segment, as the legs of pants are quite long. This case requires a dividing seam at the knee in order to cut the leg at the required length. Dividing lines can have a nice visual touch to them.

Draw a new dividing line with seam allowances onto the pattern. Each pattern line requires an extra seam allowance. Dividing seams for the knees can run straight, at an angle, or, as was common in the 1980s, with a pointed V-shape.

The legs of the pants are only cut to their final length after wearing them for a few days. Knee folds will have formed by that time, the pants therefore become slightly shorter and can now be cut to their correct length.

The best method for doing this is to wear shoes while standing on a table. A second person can mark the ideal length. In the case of thick leather, the leg is cut without the addition of a seam allowance. It is not necessary to fold, sew or glue a fold, as leather does not fray. Pants made from thinner leather should be left 2-3 cm longer and glued with a flexible glue which stays elastic. Use a rubber mallet to flatten the edge of the fold.

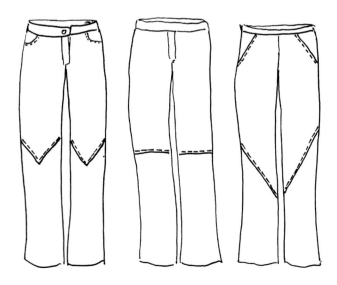

Three variations of division

3.11 **Shoes**

Shoes are among the earliest clothing of humans. The wearing of shoes had the effect that they did not have to constantly look down to check where they were stepping. They could raise their heads and walk upright, quickly and assuredly, without having to worry about thorns, underbrush, stones, heat or cold. The first shoes were most likely made from an a hide from a hunted animal which was tied around the foot, or a piece of bark tied with some bast fiber to protect the soles and to warm them. No detailed timelines for their appearance exist. Prehistoric cave paintings from 15,000 to 12,000 BC show the depiction of boots, or at least a form of foot garment with the shape of a calf protector. The oldest conserved shoes were found in 1991 in the Ötztal Glacier. Ötzi, the famous glacier mummy, was living some 5,300 years ago and was wearing leather, straw-lined drawstring shoes.

The invention of tanning leather opened up the development of a proper shoe manufacture. At first, the craftsman made both the leather and the shoes, but later the jobs were divided into tanner and shoe maker. Early historical finds and pictorial renditions prove that the working of leather and the manufacturing of shoes in particular were highly developed in ancient times. The ancient Egyptians knew about tanning methods based on minerals, plants, and oils some 8,000 years ago. During the 18th dynasty (1552-1303 BC) the quality of leather was drastically improved. The images in the tomb of Rekhmire in Thebes show the different tools and work stages involved in making shoe soles and leather threads (see page 13). At first, the sandals were rather simple. They consisted of a sole which was held in place with a system of threads, with one of them passing between the big toe and the second toe, as can be seen on the drawing. With time, shapes became more varied, particularly the instep and the top sides of the soles exhibited rich decorations. Sandals were worn to protect the feet as well as for ceremonial or representational purposes. Thus the shoes had the purpose of adornment apart from that of protection, and initially this was reserved for particular

Shoe maker tweaking the
upper leather

The opank can be found in geographic areas with stony terrains. A rectangular piece of sole is perforated at its edges and at the tip and tied or sewn at the inseam. The sole is bent at the edge and hence protects the side of the foot as well. A typical opank is the moccasin.

The half shoe is primarily used in temperate climate zones. It consists of a sole and a closed upper section called the upper. If the upper is extended over the ankle, calf, or even higher, it is called a boot.

The slipper is a shoe with a toe cap but without a heel counter, originating from ancient Persia.

groups of the population. In Egypt, at the time of about 3000 BC, this symbol of power and dignity was reserved for gods and pharaohs.

The early cultures of Mesopotamia added a heel counter to the sandal, and so the shoe was developed. During the latter Assyrian era (1048-612 BC), the shaft of the shoes was increased and hence provided more protection and firmness while riding, hunting, and going to war. The boot had a drawstring at the top and had no separate sole yet.

Due to the various needs based on climatic and geographic as well as functional and decorative aspects, many different kinds of shoes were developed. The term shoe includes all garments for the foot, which is divided into five basic types: sandal, opank, slipper, low shoe, and boot.

The sandal only protects the sole of the foot in warm areas or seasons. The sole consists of a firm piece of rawhide, leather, wood, plastic, etc. which is tied to the foot with leather threads, bands, bast fibers or similar.

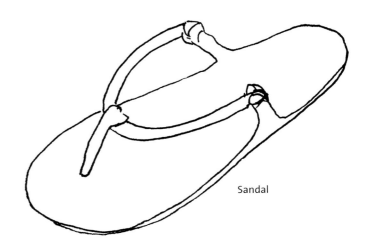

Sandal

3.12 **Slippers**

Slippers have a long history. In English the name can be traced to the 15th century, and during the 16th century, regular shoes were also called slippers if they were made from fabrics, not from leather. Only from the mid-17th century on we understand slippers to be a low shoe without tongue or heel counter leather. At that time, slippers were not only used inside homes, but they were worn with high cork heels by women on the street. They soon became a common shoe when a flat leather sole was added. During the 18th and 19th century, women wore slippers only in their home. Today, they are increasingly used outdoors again.

The oriental leather slippers with their typical upwardly curving tip are particularly beautiful and comfortable.

Tip: Test slippers can easily be sewn from industrial felt. Glue some latex to the soles so they don't slip (pun not intended).

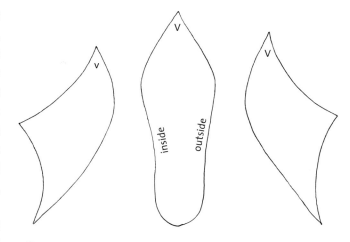

a

Material and tools
design pattern (a)
firm and robust leather (calf or medium-hard cow leather)
sole leather (vegetal-tanned cow leather)
1 to 2 cm thick foam pad (or thick felt pad), about 25 x 30 cm
matching thread
glue
sewing machine, or two leather needles when sewing by hand

Work stages

1　Enlarge the design pattern to its desired size, or use one from a slipper that fits well. Trace the pattern sections with tissue paper and mark its inside and outside lines.

2　Cut the soles once each from the top leather and the firm sole leather. Each sole receives an inlet of foam or felt. This inlet is cut all around its periphery according to the sole cut, only 7 mm smaller. Glue the centered foam inlet onto the sole leather, and on top of it, glue the sole section made from top leather. (b and c)

3　Incise the seam allowances of the entrances of the top leather, fold over and sew the edges. (d)

4　In case you want to adorn with contrasting leather colors, sew it onto the top sections now. (e)

5　Sew together at the center seam, one inner and outer top piece each.

6　Fix the top part to the sole. First, fix the slipper parts with glue. Next, sew the top part narrowly from its tip around its periphery to the sole until returning to the tip again. With this work stage, the tip of the slipper bends upwards. (f and g)

7　Once finished, cut off extra sole leather. (h)

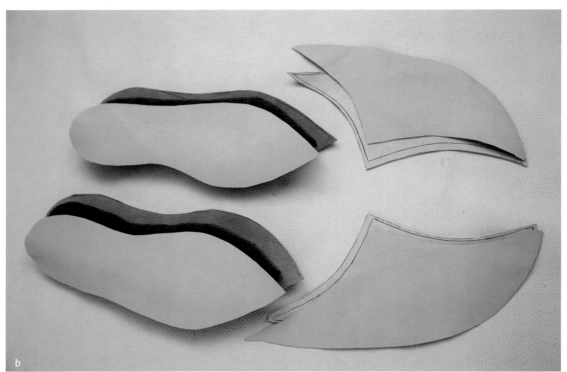

b

c

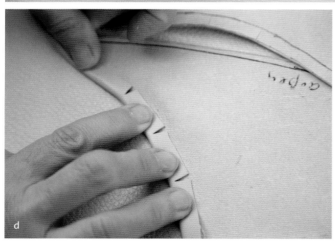

d

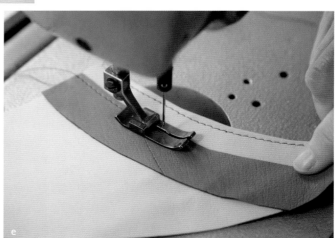

e

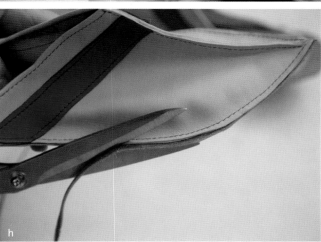

Variant: sewing by hand

Some consumer-type sewing machines are overextended when dealing with thick leather, despite a top transport and a leather needle. It is advisable to apply an old shoe maker's trick here:

1. Determine the stitch distances with a marking wheel and pre-drill the holes with an awl. Close the top center seam with two needles and thread using the saddler stitch (see page 67).
2. Next, unite the top section with the sole: from the tip, and using the running stitch, sew to the rear center, leave extra thread loose, use a second thread to sew the side of the slipper (also starting at the tip) together. Complete the seams from the rear center by performing the counter stitches (see saddler stitch, page 67). Pay attention so that the threads inside the holes, where a thread is already present, cross evenly. This is achieved by, for example, always sewing upwards on the right side and sewing down on the left, causing a rope-like seam. This work stage causes the tip of the slipper to bend upwards.

Tip: These slippers look particularly oriental if they are painted. Use leather paint in jars for this purpose, together with a small, firm brush. If you want to achieve an even pattern on all four top sections you need a pattern made from carton or brown paper with the shape of the top shoe design. Use the awl to transfer the pattern onto each top section. Use your judgement to apply smaller adornments and elements. Paint before sewing.

3.13 **Moccasin**

Moccasins are the ancient footwear of the North American natives. Its original type with its lateral flaps was usually worked from one piece of soft deer leather. Only two seams are required to make a shoe. The center seam is closed above the instep and a second seam closes the moccasin at the heel. The seams were originally covered with embroidery made from dyed pig bristles, later with small glass beads.

There is no distinction between left and right moccasin. However, it is advisable to always wear the moccasins on the same side. Soft deer leather quickly takes the shape of the foot and makes for a left and right moccasin by itself.

Material and tools
one office-size sheet of paper for the pattern
deer leather, or thick, soft velour leather, about 34 x 60 cm
measuring tape
sewing machine
awl
leather needle
matching thread

Work stages

1. put the sheet of paper on the floor and trace the center line
2. place your feet one centimeter left and right from the center line and trace them with a pen or pencil.
3. add one centimeter seam allowance to the top section of the foot. Draw the design according to the drawing and cut it out.
4. The A-B line corresponds to the circumference of the foot, which should be checked with a tape at the foot itself.
5. Place the pattern onto the leather piece and cut it out.
6. Sewing: fold the leather along the C-D line to the top side.
7. Sew from D to AB. Lock the thread at beginning and end.
8. Close the heel seam while leaving the rear seam of both flaps and 3 cm to C open. Cut open the seam allowance at the beginning of the flap until the seam.
9. Turn the moccasin inside out.
10. Close the rear flap back side to back side.
11. Try on the moccasin, mark the heel and topstitch.
12. Sew both ends at the heel and cut out the intermediate piece.
13. Cut small triangles at the seam allowance in the periphery of the tip.
14. Sew the second moccasin in the same manner.

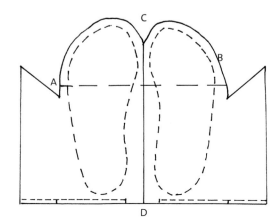

4

Handbags

A bag is an essential accessory. Back in the times of hunter gatherers, humans were looking for a way to transport their things. There are theories saying that collecting and storing things contributed to straighten the gait of man. He gained a better position to survey the scene for food and to spot possible attackers. Those who collected, usually women, had a good reason to walk upright as they had to carry plenty of things, namely their children, the collected food, and perhaps even tools. To facilitate the process of collecting food, containers and methods for carrying children and transporting food had to be developed, because due to the loss of body hair, the children could not keep themselves on their mother's back by grabbing here hair. Also, due to the upright gait, there were no skin folds where small items could be kept. Containers could make up for these shortcomings. They took off weight from hands and arms. Perhaps these containers were made from a simple large leaf or from a piece of raw hide. Due to the organic composition of these items, they have not been preserved.

In the Middle Ages, bags and pouches were carried on the belt, mostly by men, comprising the typical outfit of those days. They were made from cloth or leather, richly adorned and ornamented, often with a cover. By the 16th century, they were no more an integral part of the general fashion. One would make his own small pouches for money or handkerchief, so the craft of bag and pouch makers died out if they did not manufacture other items.

Around 1800, a bag made of cloth which matched the clothing was en vogue. During the 1930s, velvet pouches were preferred, usually made by the ladies themselves, according to manufacturing manuals.

Bags played a particularly important role with the changing social status of women in western society around 1900. The emancipation of women and the corresponding increase of working women required that they have bags for their money, keys, papers, and cosmetic items.

Ironing pouch from leather with iron clasp and textile bordure; Germany, 16th century, © Deutsches Ledermuseum-Schuhmuseum Offenbach

In addition to that, the way in which bags are carried has changed over time. Whereas during the Middle Ages it was attached to the belt, small and neat, the predominantly large bags were held firmly in hand or over the arm during the 19th and 20th century. Today, mostly large bags are carried over the shoulder or the back.

The use of a container is part of our daily life, whether it be a rucksack, suitcase, handbag, schoolbag or briefcase, or a plastic bag or shopping cart. The collecting nomad became a shopper and traveler.

Bag making comprises all types of bags, folders, covers, and pouches, small and large containers made from leather or other material. All kinds of synthetics, printed fabrics, types of felt, and other materials have somewhat displaced the traditional use of leather. Bag leather should be sturdy, soft, pliable, and elastic. The differences in quality are dependent on the type of hide, the tanning method and the dye (see chapter 1).

There is an unlimited range of variety in bag designs. In order to find your way through the jungle of a thousand possibilities, here are a few thoughts:

The Purpose	Will the bag be used on a daily basis and should it be as practical as possible, or should it be something special that com bines with a particular outfit?
Kind and Shape	Should it be a hand bag, a shoulder bag with a long carrying belt, or a rucksack?
Features	Do you need a case for your cell phone, keys or wallet? Should the bag have a broad bottom or extra-strong handles?
Size	how large or how small is the bag to be?
Design	Could the bag be an eye-catcher or should it blend harmoniously with the clothing? You need to consider the color, finish and decorative elements.

The bags which are presented in this chapter are relatively simple in design. The design patterns should be the basis for very personal creations. After making a few bags, the ideas come by themselves and the design and layout of new models becomes increasingly fascinating.

Before starting a bag project you should read thoroughly through the necessary work stages. The designs of the bags are easily enlarged or downsized with a copy machine. Adornments of all types can be added or not according to your taste. The individual projects are accompanied by recommendations concerning the leather to be used. However, you should trust your own taste when touching leather while shopping around. In order to reduce the weight on your shoulders, check that the leather is not too heavy.

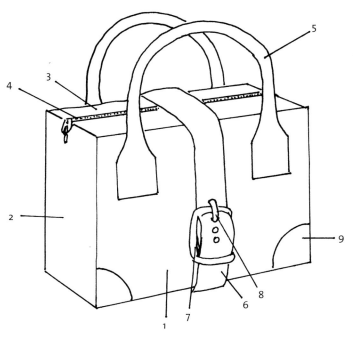

Anatomy of a bag			
1	Front section	6	Strap
2	Side section	7	Metal loop
3	Collar	8	Dome buckle
4	Zipper	9	Application
5	Handle		

Bag lining

Bags with a matching and well-finished lining are particularly attractive. Depending on the type of bag, velour leather, synthetic leather, or a nice textile lining are suitable. Leather lining is easy to work into the bag due to its firm texture. Usually it needs to be ironed to lie flat and even. Synthetic lining is great for shopper bags since it is washable. When using a textile lining, it is best to sew a strip of top leather to the handles so they are more durable. The lining can also be fitted with handy things like a cell phone pocket, key rings, or inner pockets.

4.1 **Cell Phone Case**

The entry model, so to speak, is the cell phone leather case. This model can be attached to the belt with either a velcro band or a belt sleeve, so the phone is always handy.

For a cell phone case you need small but fairly firm leather scraps, for example those from a bag. If the leather is too thin or unattractive, the case can be lined. Pig velour or felt are suitable liners. In order to keep the manufacturing as simple as possible, the outside and the lining leathers are directly glued together across their surfaces, without in-between layers. Use a rubber solution or a non-hardening glue so that the leather will not turn stiff, and to maintain its natural flexibility.

Material and tools
suitable design (a)
top leather
lining leather or felt
rubber solution or flexible glue
5 cm velcro band (auto-adhesive)
matching thread
sewing machine

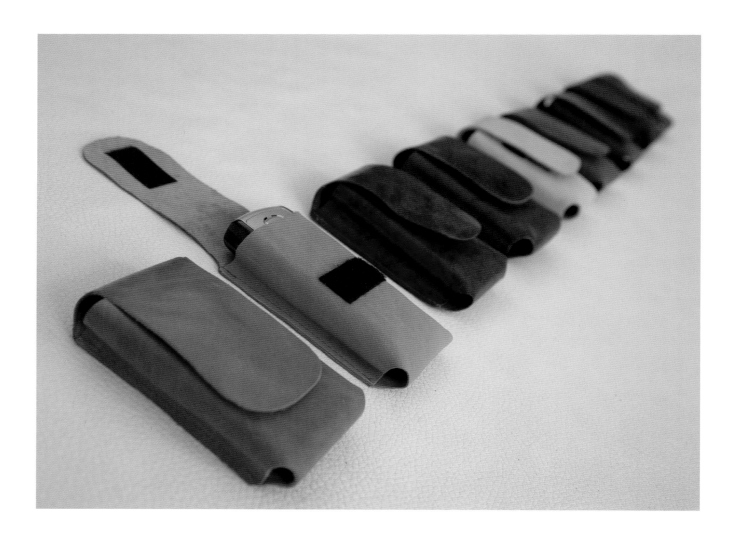

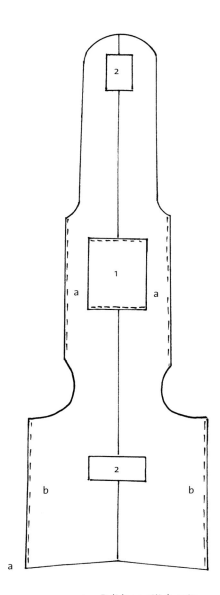

1 Belt loop, stitch onto outer side

2 Velcro strap, glue the upper part to the inner side, the lower part to the outer side

Work stages

1 All cell phones have different dimensions. This case was made for the smaller models, however, the design can easily be enlarged. Simply cut the pattern along the center line and glue a strip with the desired width in between. The belt sleeve and velcro band stay the same and are sewn or glued-on centered.

2 Make the pattern from brown paper and place it onto the top leather. Add a seam allowance of 0.5 cm and cut the leather piece along this line.

3 Cut the lining leather or felt according to the same pattern, but add an allowance of 1-2 cm to its periphery.

4 Put glue evenly on both the back side of the top leather and of the lining. Press both parts firmly together. Place a piece of paper onto the leather and rub it with your palm. When both pieces are united without any bubbles, leave them to dry for at least one hour while placing heavy books on top of them.

5 Trim away the rim of the dry leather.

6 Glue and sew the belt sleeve at its top and bottom onto the marked positions.

7 Turn the case inside out, a to b, and topstitch the lateral seams. Lock the thread ends. (b)

8 Glue the velcro band to its position and perhaps sew it on as well.

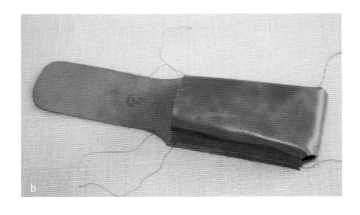

4.2 Pencil Case

The pencil case offers many possibilities to make effective use of leather scraps. The combination of felt and leather is particularly interesting. As the required piece of leather is relatively small and manageable, different techniques like appliqués, patchwork, or simply the use of leather scraps can be tried out.

Material and tools

pattern (21 x 25 cm) (a)
leather scraps
matching felt or thick, black molton
rubber lace or heddle, 1 cm width, 45 cm length
binding tape (leather, cord, etc.), 50 cm length
matching thread
sewing machine

Work stages

1 Make the pattern from brown paper and fold it lengthwise to obtain the center line. Mark it and spread the pattern again.

2 Place the pattern onto the felt and trace its outline with chalk and add an additional 1 cm to its outline. Mark the center line with chalk on its top side and cut out the felt. (b)

3 Pin the rubber heddle onto the center line of the felt with varying sizes of loops for thick pens, markers or rulers. In order to roll the case up nicely, leave the first and last 4 cm flat, without loops.

4 Sew with a tight and fine zigzag stitch (buttonhole position) each loop, not cutting the thread each time but pulling it out a little and then sewing the following loop. Only but the thread once all loops have been sewn. (d)

5 Assemble color matching leather scraps the size of the design. Once you are satisfied, glue the individual scraps at their edges. (e)

6 Place the pattern on top, mark the edges and cut out with 1 cm of seam allowance. (f)

7 Stitch the leather scraps together. Do not lock the beginning and end of the seam with back stitches, but leave some 10 cm for knotting it together. If necessary, cut away superfluous leather with fine scissors. (g)

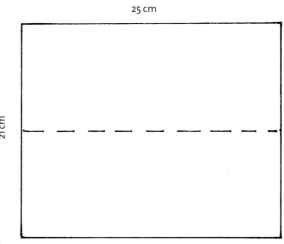

25 cm

21 cm

a

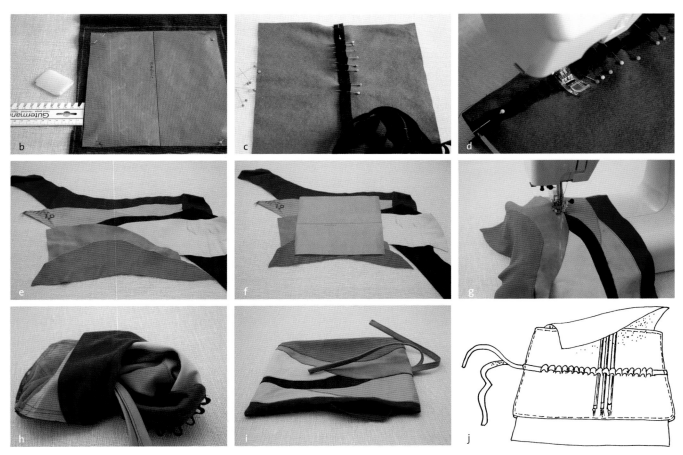

8   Put together the leather piece and felt or molton top side to top side within the seam allowance. Place a centrally folded binding tape between leather and molton at the center of a short side section so that only the fold of the tape remains visible. Stitch around with 1 cm of seam allowance, leaving an opening of 6 cm on the long side. Don't forget to lock the thread at the tip and end.

9   Cut back the four corners of the seam allowance. Turn the case inside out through its opening. (h and i)

10   Pull the seams apart and sew narrowly their circumference. This also closes the opening.

Tip: Since neither leather nor felt fray at the cut edges, the case can also be sewn together back side to back side. This is a better choice if the leather is very thick or firm.

Tip: The same method can be used for a brush case (broader) or a tool bag (larger) by changing the size of the design pattern. (j) In this case, it is advisable to add two flaps at the short sides so the tools do not slip out. The flaps, just like the binding tape, are placed between both layers of top leather and lining at the long sides before sewing them together, and are topstitched with the rest.

4.3 **Book Cover**

In order to protect beautiful books, they can be bound with leather. A leather binding is particularly useful for items which are used on a daily basis, such as notebooks, calendars, a diary, or an address book. This book cover is simple, but many different adornment techniques can be used (see chapter 6).

Material and tools

leather piece, slightly larger than the opened book

matching thread

sewing machine

punch iron

Work stages

1   Place the opened book onto the leather piece and add 1 cm of seam allowance at the top and bottom edge.
2   Close the book and wrap the leather around the book cover. For the fold to the sides, add 15 cm; 5 cm each are intended to slide the book cover into, the rest is for the latch. Cut out the leather.
3   If desired, adorn the leather.
4   Open the book again and mark the lateral seam lines and sew them. (a and b)
5   Cut a leather strip of 20 cm length and 2 cm width, fold lengthwise back to back, glue and stitch together.
6   Use the punch iron to make four holes into the latch of the book cover.
7   Place the book into the cover and run the leather band through the holes and tie together.

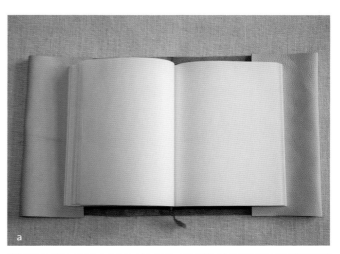

Flap Bag

This roomy bag is perfect for people with a good sense for practical things, because this bag, due to its long carrying strap, can be carried diagonally. The basic and useful pattern can be altered with personal changes such as buckles, buttons, or other adornments. The bag shown is made of lamb nappa, as this is a fine leather and very suitable for appliqués. If the bag is to be made without appliqués, it is better to choose more firm calf or cow leather. Depending on the thickness and flexibility of the leather, this bag may need a ironed-in vliseline/interfacing layer over its entire surface.

Material and tools

design pattern (a)

lamb nappa, about 5 sq. ft

leather scraps in matching colors

small thread or nail scissors

glue

vliseline LE 420 and H 250 or interfacing

firm vliseline/interfacing for carrying strap

matching thread

lining fabric (firm lining silk, cotton, perhaps flannel; here: synthetic leather), about 45 cm

possibly a belt strap, 5 cm width, 120 cm length

velcro band

sewing machine

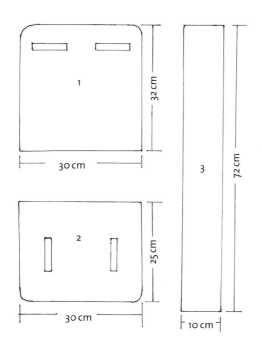

a

Work stages

1 Iron the vliseline/interfacing onto the entire back or fleshy side of the leather. Vliseline type LE 420 or interfacing is ironed with the "1" position, type H 250 with position "2"; before starting out, make an ironing test with a piece of scrap. Place the interfacing with its brilliant (glue) side onto the leather and run iron evenly some eight seconds across each section until leather and interfacing are united. The leather is now much more firm, and it also looses its stretching characteristics.

2 Make the design pattern from brown paper. (a)

3 Check the leather for possible flaws and mark them on the back side, the interfacing side. Taking into account the flaw marks, lay out the pattern on the interfacing and trace the outlines with chalk. Add 1 cm of seam allowance and cut the pattern section along these lines.

4 Cut a leather strip of 12 x 100 cm (including seam allowance) for the carrying strap; put it together from several sections of leather.

5 Appliqué: make a drawing of the original-sized appliqué on tissue paper or brown paper and cut it out. Transfer this pattern onto a fitting leather piece and cut it out. Place the appliqué onto the top side of a flap section and fix it with a thin layer of glue. Use the teflon presser foot on the sewing machine to topstitch the appliqué narrowly onto the flap. Cut off superfluous leather with small thread or nail scissors.

Tip: small irregularities are less visible if the thread is of the same color as the appliqué.

6 Glue the velcro band according to the marking onto the second flap (1) and stitch it. Place both flaps (1) top side to top side and stitch circumference while leaving an opening of 10 cm at the rear, straight side. (b) Cut out small triangles from the seam allowance

at the rounded sections. The opening is used to turn the bag flap inside out. Pull seams apart, tuck seam allowances of the opening inside and topstitch the flap narrowly.

7   From the lining fabric or synthetic leather, cut out the pattern section (2) twice, section (3) once, with a 1 cm seam allowance. Place the lining's front section (2) next to the lining's lateral section (3). At the rounded part of section (2), pinch and stitch the seam allowance at the lateral section (3). Place the rear lining (2) onto the other side of the lateral section (3), pinch and stitch.

8   Put together the leather parts for the outer bag in the same way as you did with the bag lining.

9   Place outer bag and bag lining into each other, top side to top side (d), line up the seams and topstitch the upper open edge around its circumference. Leave some 10 cm at the rear edge to be able to turn it later. (e) Incise the seam allowance at its edges up to the seam; pull all seam allowances apart and perhaps glue them on. Turn the bag inside out, tuck the seam allowance of the opening inwards and topstitch narrowly, closing the opening this way.

10   Glue the velcro band according to the design onto the front side of the outer bag and topstitch through both layers, outer layer and lining. Outer bag and lining are now united.

11   Glue the bag flap to the rear (1) part of the bag and topstitch.

12   To strengthen the carrying strap, iron firm interfacing onto the fleshy side, fold the strap top side to top side lengthwise and stitch the long edges. Use a knitting needle or a straight stick to turn the strap inside out. Fold the strap so that the seam lies exactly in the center of the strap, then stitch narrowly around circumference. Affix the belt strap to the carrying strap. Sew the carrying strap to the lateral sections (3) of the bag.

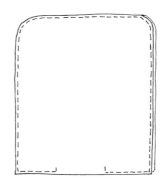

b

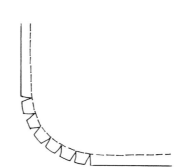

c

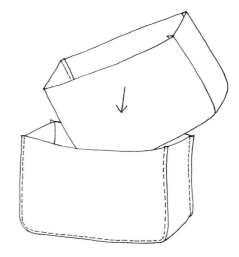

d

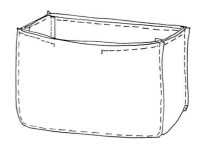

e

Evening Bag I / II

Often a small bag with the basics is enough for the evening. These two bags made from goat leather are small and neat. They are made from the same basic design but feature distinctive details. The carrying strap of the lime green bag is designed to be used as a belt as well, which is why it can be adjusted with a small buckle. This gives you complete freedom of movement of the arms, even while dancing.

Bag I (blue)

Material and tools
design (a)
goat leather
lining fabric, 50 cm
2 zippers in matching colors: 20 cm length for top closure; 12 cm for inner bag
interfacing for belt (1 cm width; 128 cm length)
matching thread
glue
sewing machine

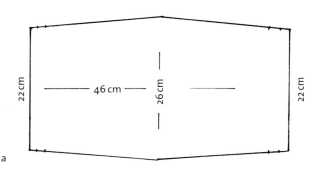

22 cm — 46 cm — 26 cm — 22 cm

a

b

Work stages

1 Make the design according to the drawing.
2 Check the leather for flaws and mark them on the back side.
3 Affix the pattern section with scotch tape onto the fleshy side of the leather and trace the outline. Add 1 cm seam allowance to the circumference and cut out along this line (b)
4 Cut two 8 x 8 cm leather pieces for the handle loops.
5 Cut the handle to a width of 3 cm and a length of 128 cm. If the leather piece is too short, put the handle together from several pieces.
6 Cut the bag lining according to the design but 0.5 cm smaller than the leather piece.
7 Cut a small inner pocket from the lining material, place the short zipper at the top and stitch. Iron the seam allowance inwards, place the inner pocket onto the top side of the bag lining and stitch (c)
8 Close the lateral seams of the lining bag. Sew the lower edges laterally as shown so that the bag becomes bulgy. (e)
9 Glue the seam allowances of the handle loops to the fleshy side and bend them around a pencil into a curved piece. (d)
10 Glue the outer bag, top side to top side, while glueing both handle loops 5 cm below the upper edge into the lateral seams. Stitch the lateral seams and include the handle loops.
11 Fold and stitch the lower edges of the outer bag at right angles, just like the lining bag.

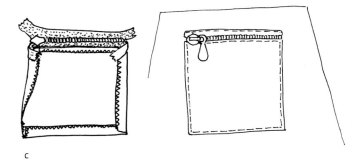

c

12 Cut away superfluous leather and turn the bag inside out. (f and g)
13 Put outer and lining bag back side to back side into each other. Glue the 20 cm long zipper to the upper edge of the leather and stitch, include the lining bag as well.
14 Iron the waistline-vliseline/interfacing to the fleshy side of the handle (do a test first). Fold the handle back to back lengthwise and stitch circumference. Pull handle ends through the handle loops and knot them together.

Bag II (lime green)

Additional material

magnetic press-button instead of the longer zipper

4 eyelets with a diameter of 11 mm

Work stages

Basically, the green bag is made just like the blue one, with the difference that instead of the long zipper, a magnetic button is used. So as not to be visible on its outer side, the back sides of the magnetic button are worked into the lining or trimming. Affix the eyelets as described on page 59. (a and b)

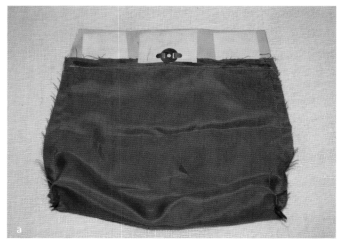

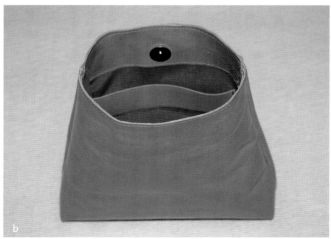

Business Bag

This bag makes for a great appearance, whether at the office or elsewhere.

A business bag is used to carry quite a bit of volume or weight, so it is best to use even, thick, tear- and stretch-resistant leather. The old-fashioned, brown business bags are made from vegetal-tanned leather. They become more beautiful with use, as the patina which forms over time makes the leather come alive. Cow leather is particularly firm and is the best choice for transporting heavy items, no matter how it is tanned. Chrome-tanned cow leather is robust and tough, and best of all, it is available in appealing colors.

Design

body including flap: a rectangle of 45 cm width and 115 cm length

lateral pieces: two rectangles, rounded at the bottom, size 12 x 25 cm

handle: two strips of 4 x 50 cm and two strips of 4 x 80 cm

crossing strap: one strip of 4 x 90 cm

Material and tools

design (a)

cow leather

lining fabric, e.g. firm cotton, 60 cm

matching thread

waistband-type vliseline/interfacing, 130 x 4 cm

2 buckles (one for the front fastener, one for the carrying strap)

zipper, 20 cm length for inner pocket inside the lining

1 press button for upper fastener

roll cutter

punch pliers

sewing machine

leather color and fine brush

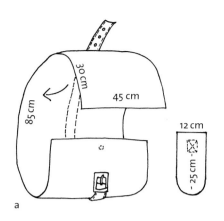

a

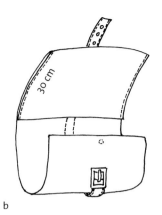

b

c

Work stages

1 Make the pattern according to the drawing (a). Place the sections onto the fleshy side of the leather, conserving surface area, trace outline, and cut without seam allowance.

2 Dye the cut edges of the circumference strap with leather dye or paint. Affix a buckle at one end of the strap and glue the strap according to the drawing onto the top side of the bag's body. The buckle is at the front side and the flap features an extended piece of the strap. Sew the strap on.

3 To line the bag flap, turn the leather over, back side to back side, some 30 cm, and topstitch at the sides. (b)

4 For the handles, iron the waistband-type vliseline/interfacing onto the fleshy side of a 50 cm long and an 80 cm long leather strip (perform a test first). Complete the straps with their counterparts, glue back to back and stitch circumference. Place one handle each some 4 cm below the top edge onto each lateral section and topstitch.

5 Glue the lateral sections with the handles onto the bag body and stitch—the seam allowances are outwards.

6 Use the second buckle to unite both handles.

7 Paint all cut edges with leather paint or dye. (d)

8 As the bag is fairly broad, it is advisable to affix a small closing flap with a magnetic button at the center of the bag's body. One part of the button is worked centered some 6 cm below the opening into the front section of the bag. Affix the button's counterpart onto a 4 x 20 cm long strip of leather.

d

9 Cut the design sections for the body at 58 cm length and 45 cm width, and the two lateral sections at 12 x 26.5 cm (all including seam allowance) from the lining fabric. If desired, sew the inner pocket onto the top side of the lining fabric.

10 Pin the lateral sections of the lining onto the long sections of the lining body and stitch with 1 cm seam allowance. Iron the seam allowances at the upper edge of the lining bag to the back side and glue the lining back to back onto the top edge of the leather bag. Glue the leather strip with the press-button centered onto the back. Stitch circumference while including the leather strip.

Small variation

For the little sister of the business bag, use the same basic design, only quite smaller, and affix the handle diagonally and without doubling it, rather, simply round it off—there you go, you get a really neat bag.

Material and tools
design pattern (a)
cow leather
waistband vliseline/interfacing: 2 x 100 cm
large buckle
two small buckles for the carrying strap
matching thread
glue
sewing machine
leather paint or dye and a fine brush

Work stages

1. Scale down the design and make sure that the flap is not laid out doubled, rather, rounded off. Cut two strips of 2 x 100 cm for the handle. (a and b)

2. Basically, proceed the same way as with the business bag, however, adjust the size for affixing the strap according to the design at step 2 and cut a slit into the flap, which is used to pull the strap through. (c and d)

3. Punch about five holes into the carrying strap at both ends. Affix one small buckle at the front, below the flap, and a second buckle, according to the design, diagonally onto the back side of the bag's body. Pull the carrying strap through the buckle.

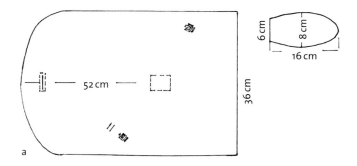

Shopper Bag

The Shopper is a roomy bag for all kinds of purchases. The two horn handles are easy on the hands, making this one particularly practical. It is quite easy to fabricate.

Material and tools
design pattern (a)
cow leather
horn handles (alternatively, from bamboo or synthetics)
glue
waistband vliseline/interfacing, 80 cm
matching thread
leather color or dye and a fine brush

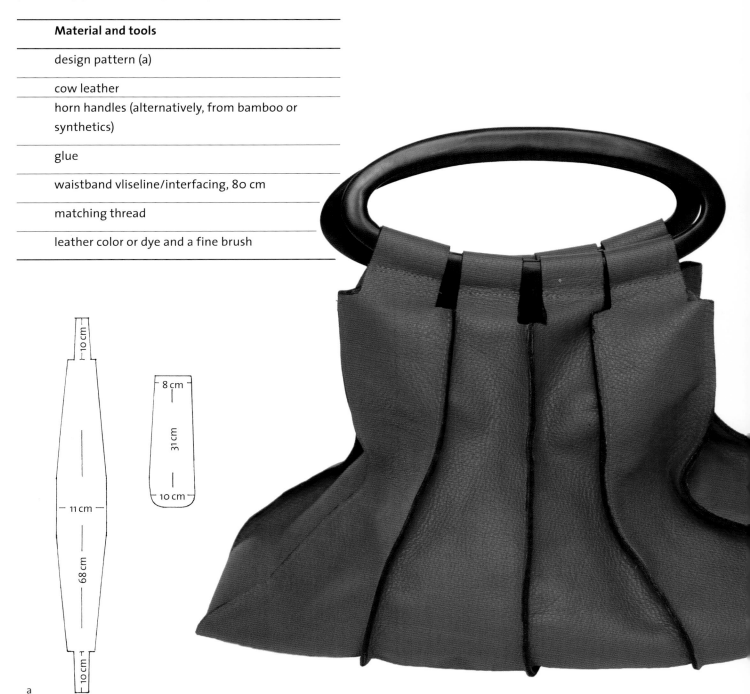

a

b

c

d

e

f

Work stages

1. Place the pattern onto the leather, minimizing cut-off, and trace the outline and add 0.5 cm of seam allowance, then cut the pieces along these lines. (b)

2. Glue the longitudinal sides of two long strips within the seam allowance back to back and stitch. Put together all the other leather strips in this manner. (c and d)

3. Glue the lateral sections within the seam allowance back to back onto the side sections and stitch. If necessary, shorten the seam allowances evenly. (e)

4. Iron onto the fleshy side of the top loops 10 cm of waistband vliseline/interfacing each, affix with glue and topstitch. Cut away excess leather.

5. Paint all the cut edges with a fine brush. (f)

Shoulder Bag

This bag with a collar offers enough space for a notebook plus its accessories, and the two straps distribute the weight on the shoulders nicely. A few neat extras, like a rounded goat leather appliqué and the stamped-out and underlaid strap ends, loosen up the box-like shape of this bag.

Design

body: one rectangle of 42 cm (width) x 60 cm (length)
lateral sections: two rectangles of 13 x 19 cm
collar: two rectangles of 6 x 57 cm
straps: two strips of 8 x 91 cm from leather and two strips of 3 x 73 cm from belt strap

Material and tools

design (a)
calf nappa leather
zipper, 60 cm long, non-divisible
leather scrap for appliqué, here: goat leather
belt strap of webbing
a plate, as a template
scalpel and punch iron
sewing machine
glue
matching thread
leather color or dye and a fine brush

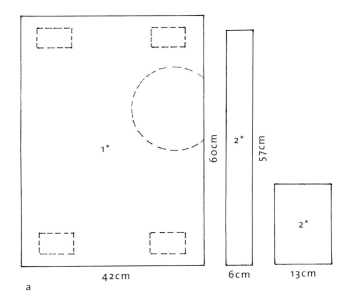

a

b

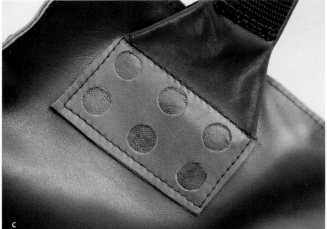

c

Work stages

1   Make the pattern and lay it out, while conserving space, onto the fleshy side of the calf leather, affix with tape and trace the outline. Add 0.5 cm of seam allowance and cut the sections along this line.

2   To make the appliqué, place a suitably-sized plate onto a leather scrap, mark the outline and cut the leather pieces with a scalpel. Glue the appliqués onto the bag's body and narrowly stitch circumference. (b)

3   Fold the straps lengthwise back to back so that the edges meet at the center of the rear. Leave about 9 cm open at each end. Glue the straps together. Cut the belt strap and glue and stitch it onto the top side of the handles.

4   Punch out the ends of the handles six times each. Place another leather scrap, colored like the appliqué, below these holes and stitch the handles onto the bag body.

5   Affix the zipper between the collar pieces so that it is visible and stitch it on.

6   Place the lateral pieces back to back onto the collar and stitch. Frame this edge with a piece of leather.

7   Glue the collar and the lateral sections onto the bag's body and stitch circumference.

8   Highlight the leather edges with leather dye or color.

Tote Bag

The basic shape of this bag, made from fine, soft calf leather, is inspired by the bag shapes and forms of Morocco. This bag is large and roomy and apt for daily use. Folders and notepads fit just as well as daily shopping items.

Material and tools

design pattern (a)

calf leather

lining fabric, i.e. cotton

adhesive strips

2 zippers, 30 cm length for the top, 18 cm for the inner pocket inside the lining

thermo-adhesive lining, the length of the handles

buckle for handles

4 metal loops, flat wire

2 snap hooks

4 eyelets to trim the holes

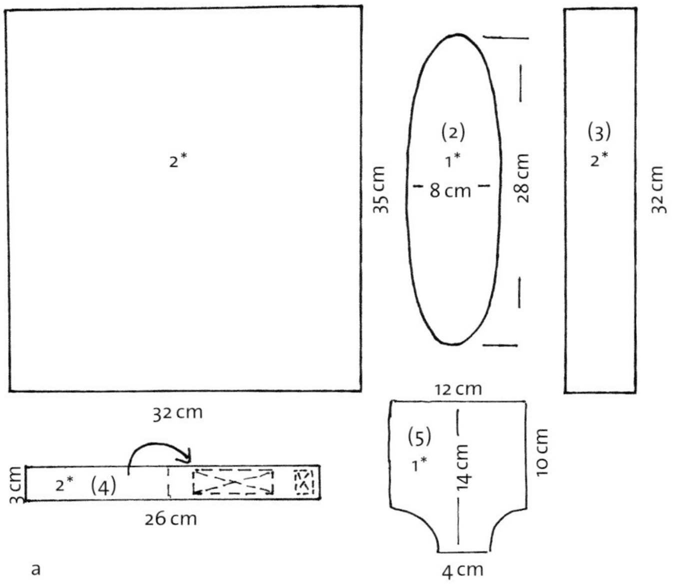

2*

32 cm

35 cm

(2)
1*
8 cm

28 cm

(3)
2*

32 cm

12 cm

(5)
1*

14 cm

10 cm

4 cm

3 cm
2* (4)
26 cm

a

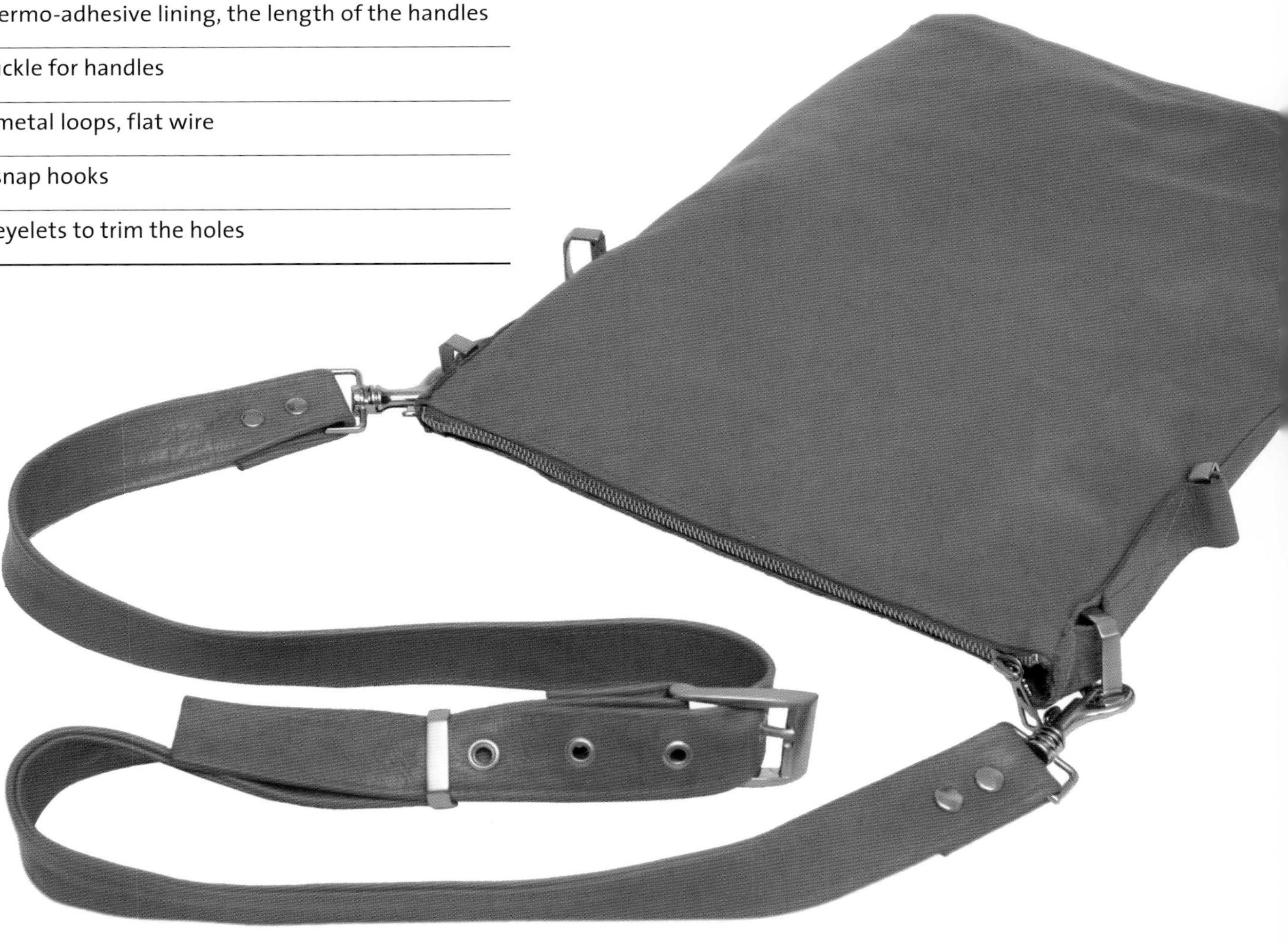

Work stages

1 Make the pattern and affix it with adhesive strips to the leather, add 0.5 cm of seam allowance and cut out the pieces along this line. (b, c and d)

2 Clamp the sections together with paper clips (1), stitch the lateral seams, fold the seam allowances apart and glue. (e, f and g)

3 Sew in the oval bottom (2). (h)

4 Make the bag lining from the same pattern, only 0.5 cm smaller at the sides and 5 cm smaller at the top. Trim all pattern sections with a zigzag or overlock stitch.

5 Sew in a covered zipper at the small lining inner pocket (see page 60), iron the seam allowances to the back side and stitch the inner pocket onto the top side of the lining bag. (i and j)

6 Stitch the leather application (3) to the top of the lining bag and affix the small cell phone case (5) to the lining. (k, l and m)

7 Cut two carrying straps of the desired length and width, iron on the interfacing to the back side while keeping in mind that anilin-tanned leather is sensitive to heat. Fold the carrying straps lengthwise and stitch circumference. Affix the buckle for changing the length of the carrying strap.

8 Sew the outer loops (4) for the carrying strap mounting laterally to the bag's body. Cut one leather strip of 3 x 26 cm each, work in two of the metal loops, according to the drawing, and stitch the leather flap with the loops onto the lateral seam of the bag's body. (n)

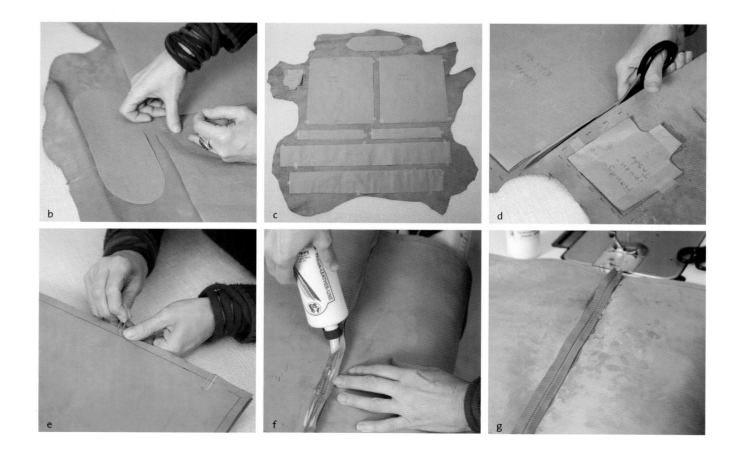

b

c

d

e

f

g

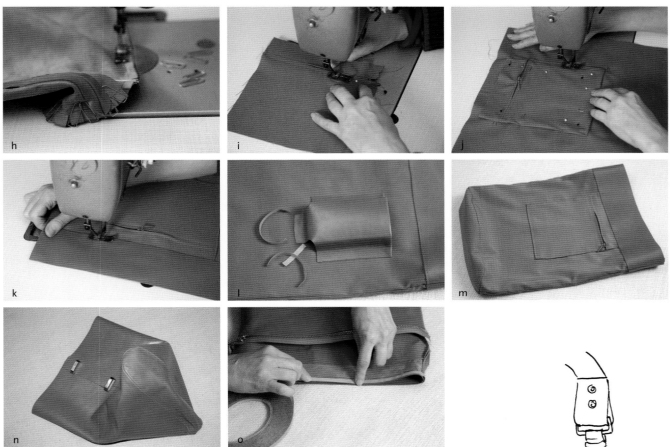

9   Place the lining bag back to back into the bag, and
     glue the zipper with scotch tape between the outer
     bag and the appliqué and sew it in, leaving it visible.
     (o)

10   Affix the snap hooks to the carrying strap and hook
     them into the metal loops. If hooked at the top, the
     bag is very roomy, if hooked at the bottom, the re-
     sult is a smaller and very flexible bag, due to the
     folding of the flap.

5

Home Accessories

Leathers and hides are popular materials for living areas. There is a good reason that many people still live in "leather houses." The wigwams and teepees of the North American natives are covered with leathers and hides, some of them also with reed and grass mats. The bell-shaped eskimo tents for use in summer are also made from leather. Leather wall paper was and is still in use today, and it is available even with a crocodile look.

Leather is an ideal material for living quarters. Designers have known this for quite some time and because of this, much furniture, like arm chairs, sofas and chairs, is covered with leather. Leather is a natural product, it is hard-wearing, keeps its form, and it also acquires a patina with a noble shine with repeated use. However, un-worked leather also contributes to the look and feel of a home, for example as a white cow leather placed on a sofa or as a rug on the floor. And how about half a cow leather as a table top, or a piece of calf leather as a mouse pad? Lamps made from natural white see-through parchment provide a warm and cozy ambience.

It has become trendy again to self-fabricate accessories, and the living area offers many possibilities for that. Cushions in all variations and sizes, including floor cushions, are particularly suitable. Cushions are great to try out adornment techniques such as leather patchwork, leather knitting or appliqués, while using leather scraps. Storage boxes are also always a handy item, as they allow to quickly store away all kinds of items. They can be made of all sizes, colors and shapes, including a firm lid. In addition, braids and special leather adornment stitches can be applied, as shown in chapter 2.

5.1 **Braided Baskets**

These braided baskets are simple, easy to make, and practical. The design is made with a long ruler and a square out of brown paper. The sizes are indicated on the drawing, however, there is a large margin for personal creations. A personalized basket can be braided by determining its size, firmness of the leather, color, and the width of the strips, according to your preferences. Both pictured baskets have the same basic design and size, however, due to the variations in color, leather firmness and width of the strips, they look completely different.

In addition to the main pattern section (a), the white basket requires three strips of 82 x 5 cm. The brown basket has a width of the braided strips that is half as wide, so six strips of 82 x 2.5 cm are required. Also, the braided strips on the drawing are only 2 cm wide for the brown basket, but there are ten of them.

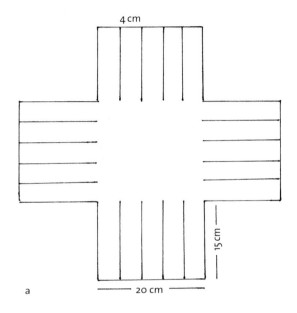

4 cm

15 cm

a

20 cm

Work stages for brown basket

1   Lay out the pattern while conserving leather, mark it on the leather and cut out along these lines.
2   Cut out the additional strips and sew them together at their narrow sides to form a ring.
3   Soak all leather parts in warm water, place them into a plastic bag and leave overnight to soak. The next day the leather will be very easy to shape, and it does not slip as easily when braiding it. (b)
4   Weave in each leather ring as shown. The higher you get while doing this, the more likely it becomes that everything slips out of place. Use clothespins, always placing them in the same manner. The pins fix the braided section, even at the last row. (c to i)
5   Leave the basket to dry overnight, then the edges can be glued piece by piece and clamped again until glue and leather are completely dry.

Variation

The white basket is made in the same manner, except that this one is made from a softer cow leather and the strips are twice as wide as those of the brown basket. It is advisable to include a piece of wire at the rim, as the basket can not hold its shape by itself.

Material and tools
design pattern (a)
vegetal-tanned cow leather
40 clothespins
sharp scissors or cutter
leather glue in a tube

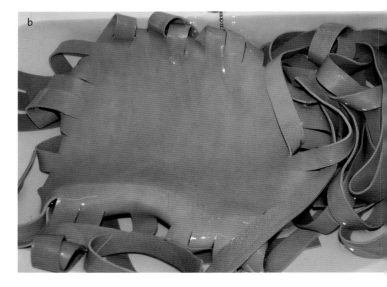

b

Hatbox

Hats require a protected place, more so if they are transported. For this purpose, round hatboxes have been around for ages, made from carton, wood or leather. Certainly a hatbox can hold many other items and provide an uncluttered, orderly home. Such a hatbox requires some time and patience, but the effort is well worth it.

Material and tools

design pattern (a)

thick and firm vegetal-tanned, non-dyed cow leather

split velour of the same size for the lining

flexible leather glue in a can

bristle brush

sharp scissors or cutter

awl

folding stick or bone

firm leather thread

2 thick needles

6 rivets

hammer

cork base

circle 1 (top) with a diameter of 25 cm

circle 2 (bottom) with a diameter of 24 cm

leather strip (top): 80 x 3 cm + 5 cm for the flap

leather strip (body): 78 x 14 cm + 5 cm for the flaps

Work stages

1   Make the pattern in the desired size.

2   Lay out the pattern sections on the cow leather, trace the outlines and cut with a cutter or sharp scissors. (a)

3   Place the pattern section onto the back side of the velour leather and also trace them, but do not cut! It is possible that the leather will stretch due to the humidity of the glue.

4   Cover the back side of the velour leather as well as the back side of the cow leather evenly with flexible glue. Always work section by section, or the glue may harden too quickly!

5   Glue the cow leather parts onto the back side of the velour leather and press flat with a folding stick. Be careful so that no bubbles or folds are formed between the leathers!

6   Place some heavy books on the patterns and leave to dry overnight. Both leathers are now firmly united.

7   To sew the seams, mark with a tape 1 cm steps at the lower edge of the body of the box, the top of the lid band, the circumference of the bottom and top, about 7 mm from the edge, and pre-drill these markings with an awl. (b)

Tip: the best way to do this is by placing a piece of cork under the leather. This makes it easy to perforate the leather with the awl while preventing the two leathers from coming apart.

8   Use the saddle stitch and double thread to sew together both leather parts.

9   When finished, punch out the holes for the right size of rivet at the leather flaps and set them with a hammer.

10 In order to prepare the box for real travel use, it gets the typical carrying strap, which also firmly closes the box.

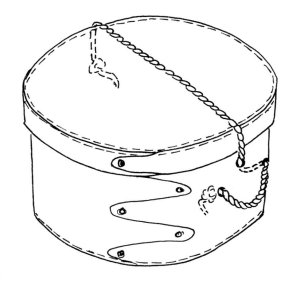

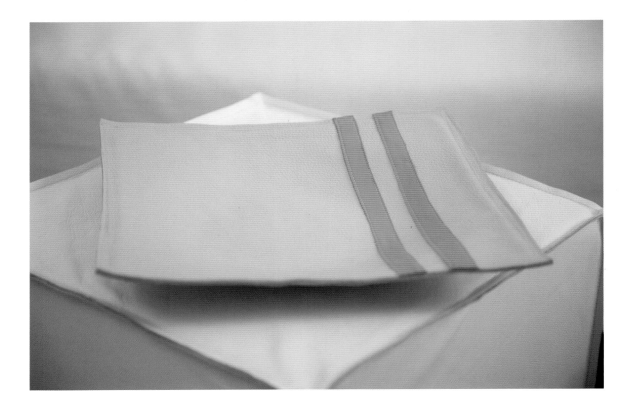

5.3 **Leather Bowl**

Many items are perfectly suited for a leather bowl: the car keys, fruit, or the knitting items in the living room. This leather bowl is made from two leather layers, with a supporting layer of paper mache in the center. The light, soft, chrome-tanned cow leather with its coarse grain provides a certain natural look to the bowl, emphasized by the patina that forms with time and use. The original shape is derived from an existing glass bowl. It was used to shape the carton center and for final shaping of the leather. It does not have to be square necessarily, and may just as well be round or oval. The work stages remain the same.

Material and tools
bowl to derive the form
leather of appropriate size
perhaps leather strips of a different color for decoration
paper glue strips from a roll
water bowl
household sponge
tissue paper
glue
bristle brush
folding stick
matching thread
sewing machine

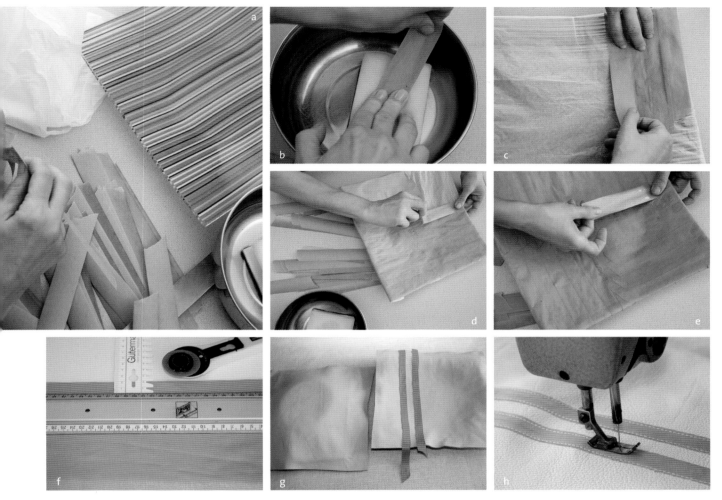

Work stages

1 Line the bowl with tissue paper.

2 Moisten paper glue strips by dragging them over the sponge, then glue them onto the tissue paper inside the bowl. You can improve the its firmness by placing several overlapping layers of strips on top of each other. About four layers should be sufficient. Then, leave the paper mache bowl to dry on the original form. (a to e)

3 Cut two leather pieces 1 cm larger than the original bowl and moisten the fleshy side with a sponge.

4 Stretch the moistened leather parts over the inside and outside of the bowl, affix them and leave to dry.

5 For decorative purposes, cut leather strips from a different color leather scrap and glue it onto the top section of the leather bowl and stitch. (f to h)

6 Remove the bowl form then glue together the leather pieces and the carton bowl over their entire surfaces and use the folding stick to press out air bubbles, then leave to dry.

7 Stitch top and bottom leather at the rim of the carton bowl and cut back extra leather to some 3 mm.

Tip: it is advisable to make a test with a piece of leather scrap beforehand. In case the leather is rather delicate, use a 1:1 spiritus-water solution and carefully spray onto the leather. Spiritus evaporates faster than water and does not leave traces.

Living Room Cube

Many people never find just the right couch table and prefer to put a tray on top of a cube. It is also great as an extra chair, an ottoman to stretch your legs, or as a decorative sofa accessory. And it is really quick to make, too.

Material and tools
design pattern, square of 41 cm length (including seam allowances)
Cow or calf leather, sufficient for 6 squares of 41 cm length
Firm foam cube, 40 x 40 x 40 cm
2 leather bands, 2 m each, of same color
glue
matching thread
sewing machine
awl or punch pliers

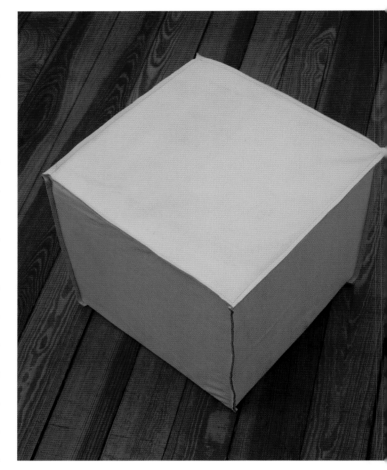

Work stages

1   Make five patterns of 41 x 41 x 41 cm and one pattern for the bottom of 40 x 40 x 40 cm, lay out on the leather and cut out.

2   Since leather has a clean cut edge and does not fray, the seam allowances can be placed outside, as shown with the pictured cube. Seam allowances can certainly lie inside as well, this decision needs to be made before step 3.

3   Sew together all four side sections, piece by piece. It is best to glue the fleshy sides at the seam allowances together to prevent slippage while sewing. Do not close the seam to the top, but stop 0.5 mm (seam allowance) before the end. When all four side sections are joined, sew on the top square. (a, b and c)

4   Cover the cube. This can be rather difficult, depending on the back side of the leather and the type of foam. Once the cube is upholstered, cut off the edges at the bottom diagonally. (d, e and f)

5   Place the bottom and perforate the edges facing the floor with an awl at 10 cm intervals. (g)

6   Matching the holes in the side edges, mark holes at the bottom and pre-drill with the awl or punch pliers.

7   Tension the bottom and side sections with the leather bands. (h and i)

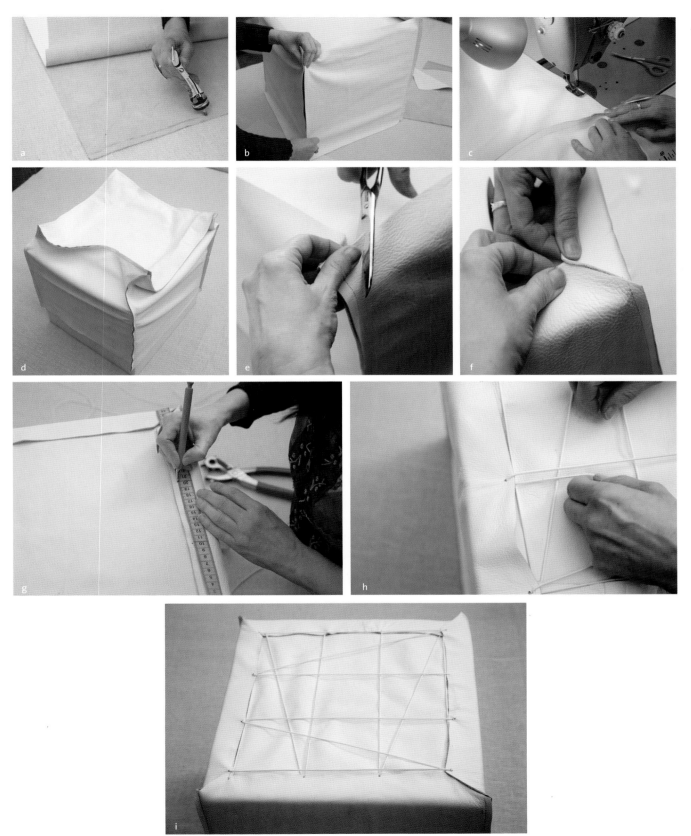

5.5 **Parchment Lamp**

Parchment is an un-tanned animal hide from goat, sheep, calf, cow, and even donkey. The hide is soaked in lime water to loosen the hair roots. Once free from hair and cleaned, it is stretched onto racks and worked on its fleshy side with scrapers until all of the loose connecting tissue has been removed. The hide is then rubbed with fine chalk and sanded and polished with pumice stones. (a)

A large portion of humanity's history has been written on parchment. It was one of the most important writing surfaces before the invention of paper. The name parchment is derived from the Mysian city of Pergamon, where parchment manufacturing was allegedly invented. However, it is more likely that the method had been known longer and that it was improved in Pergamon. A legend transmitted by Pliny of Varro says that parchment was discovered because Ptolemy Epiphanes of Egypt stopped the export of papyrus, the most common writing material. This is how parchment was developed in Pergamon, soon surpassing papyrus as a better alternative. It was more flexible and durable and had the advantage that it could be sanded and reused. After Alexandria, Pergamon had the largest library of antiquity.

a

b

Towards the end of the Middle Ages, parchment was increasingly displaced by paper. Parchment is still used today for drum skins and for the manufacture of lamps, which, due to their transparency, provide a beautiful warm and mild light. Stability is provided by e.g. aluminum bars. If the parchment is slightly perforated with incisions, a play of light is projected into the entire room.

Material and tools

parchment (here: goat), whitened, about 5.2 sq. ft

lamp set with bulb holder, suspension, cord, switch and bulb

3 aluminum poles, 1 m long, 2 mm thick

paper clips

scalpel

awl

firm thread, creme-colored

thick needle

pliers

Work stages

1   Roll the parchment lengthwise into a cylinder of 80 cm circumference. Tie a firm thread around the roll. Clamp the parchment at its top and bottom with paper clips.

2   The frame is composed of three aluminum poles or rods. The poles are affixed with the help of two small slits of 6 mm length, 1 cm apart, cut into the parchment. Measure the center of the hide (half the lamp's height is equivalent to the animal's spine line) and mark three spots for the slits, some 27 cm apart. From these points, go 20 cm towards the top and bottom and mark a slit there as well. Make the total of nine small loops (three each) by cutting the slits and thread the aluminum poles from the inside. (b and c)

3   To permanently fix the parchment roll, make a cross stitch seam at the center of each overlap. Stabilize the roll and mark and pre-drill twelve holes, six under each other, spaced 2 cm apart. Starting on the top left, sew the cross stitches with a firm thread. Knot the end of the thread. (d)

4   Arrange the aluminum poles so that the entire parchment cylinder almost touches the ground. Use the pliers to cut back the aluminum poles to the desired length.

5   The light source is a ready-made lamp set from a dealership, including a low-watt lamp, which is covered by the parchment cylinder, without any additional fixture.

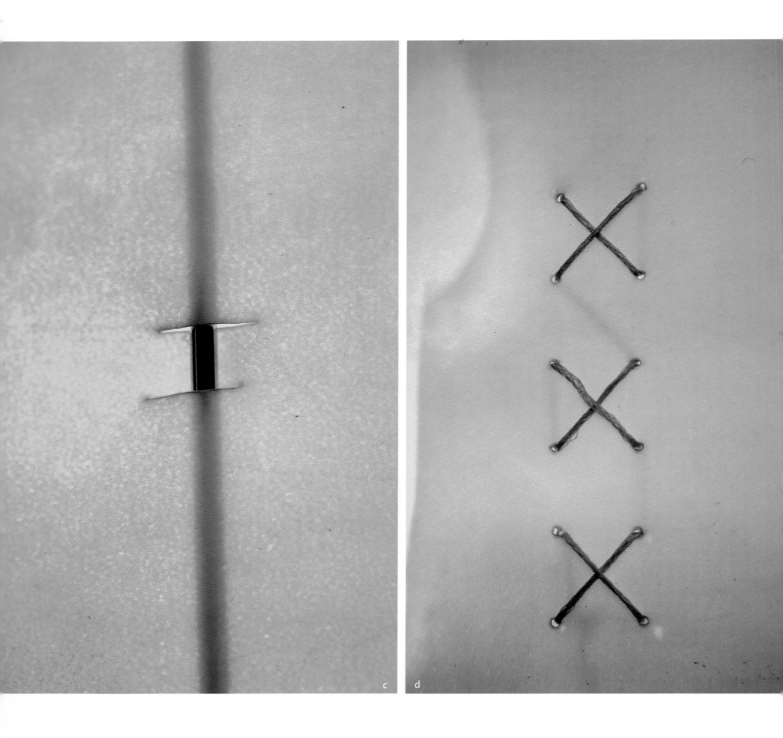

5.6 **Cushion with Appliqué**

Cushions and pillows are always pleasant as home accessories, and they can be designed quite attractively. An interesting look results from the combination of different materials, such as leather and felt. Leather has been used since ancient times to strengthen items made from felt, making it more durable and resistant. In addition, the contrast between the two archaic and natural materials is quite appealing. The structure and treatment of leather and felt have many things in common, which is not too surprising as both are derived from animals.

You can use a small felt cushion to try out the combination of the two materials. The pictured cushion is only 30 x 30 cm.

Material and tools

wool felt, New Zealand merino wool, pictured in magenta color, about 200 gr.

two bubble wrap pieces of film (one of 50 x 50 cm, one of 50 x 100 cm)

hot soapy water

spray bottle

a little vinegar

iron

pressing cloth

leather scraps (shown: fine pink calf leather)

flexible glue

thread of same color as leather

measuring tape

sewing machine

2 matching buttons

Work stages

Felt cushion:

1 Lay out the two wool felt sections, one for the front side, about 40 x 40 cm, the other one is used to make the back side of the cushion, including its closure, 40 x 55 cm. (a)

2 Place the smaller piece of wool felt without any holes and with an even thickness onto the large bubble wrap pane. Spray evenly with hot soapy water (one tablespoon of neutral soap per liter) and cover it with the second pane of bubble wrap. (b)

3 Press the soapy water with light, circular movements into the felt. You can tell that the water has been evenly absorbed by the felt when its thickness is uniform and when it is darker in color, as all air has been expelled from it; roll up the wool felt between the bubble wrap and carefully roll it back and forth. Open the roll after two minutes and carefully stretch out and flatten any folds and creases. (c and d)

4 Turn everything 90 degrees and roll up the surface once more. Roll it for three minutes, unroll it, flatten creases, turn another 90 degrees and roll up again, etc. Apply more pressure with each pass. If tongues appear at the corners, which is due to uneven pressure while rolling, stretch the felt diagonally and roll it up from the corners.

5   Now and then, check the size with the tape measure. Once the surface is about 30 x 30 cm, rinse the felt with water. To neutralize the soap, add a dash of vinegar into the last water while rinsing, then iron the felt surface (position 2) with a pressing cloth and pull it into shape. Leave to dry and then felt the second pane for the back side.

Leather appliqué:

1   Cut shapes and motifs for the appliqué from leather scraps. (e)
2   Glue the appliqué onto the face side of the cushion and narrowly topstitch the circumference. Finish by pulling the thread ends to the rear side and knot them together. (f, g and h)
3   Cut away superfluous leather from the appliqué edges with small scissors.
4   Cut the rear section of the cushion into two parts, incise the button holes, sew on the buttons and sew together both felt sections, top side to top side. (i and j)

5·7 **Patchwork Cushion**

The patchwork technique was born from necessity. Usable sections of old clothing were cut out and patched together again. In addition, patchwork clothing used to also be a sign of wealth and status. In times when there was no printing or elaborate dyeing of clothes, patching together individual pieces was the only way to make clothing a little more colorful and interesting.

Leather patchwork is an excellent opportunity to make use of scrap leather while adding color to an item. The following are two simple instructions for making patchwork cushions and pillows:

Patchwork I

A simple patchwork pattern where only squares are needed to form a face.

Material and tools

design pattern: carboard pattern 12 x 12 cm

leather scraps of various colors, at least 12 x 12 cm

thread

sewing machine

wool felt, New Zealand merino wool in matching color, about 100 gr.

spray bottle

2 bubble wrap panes (one of 70 x 140 cm, one of 70 x 70 cm)

hot water

neutral soap

measure tape

a little vinegar

iron

pressing cloth

leather buttons

Work stages

1 Make the carboard pattern of 12 x 12 cm (with 1 cm seam allowance each).
2 Cut leather squares of 12 x 12 cm, 25 total. Smaller leather scraps can be sewn together in three pieces of 12 x 4 cm each to form a square. The pictured cushion consists of the following squares: 8 x dark red, 6 x red, 6 x orange, 5 x beige.
3 Arrange the squares evenly, always five per row. (a)
4 Glue the squares onto each other for the first row, top side to top side. All seam allowances are glued in the same direction.
5 Sew the second row in the same way, only glue and sew the seam allowances in the other direction.

8   Cut the felt at the center into two parts of 50 x 30 cm, incise the button holes and sew on the buttons (here, covered with leather). You can cover buttons with leather yourself (see page 60) or have them covered.

9   Button the felt pieces together and place them top side to top side onto the leather piece, inside of the seam allowance. Stitch the circumference of the cushion's front and rear side together.

10   Cut the edges of the seam allowances at an angle, open the buttons and turn the cushion lining inside out.

6   When all five rows have been sewn together, sew the strips of squares together. Make sure that the corners meet. (b)

7   Evenly lay out the rectangular wool felt of 65 x 80 cm on the large bubble wrap pane and felt its back side as described for the cushion with appliqué until the surface measures some 50 x 60 cm.

Patchwork II

The second cushion is done just like the first one, only that instead of leather squares, leather strips of 52 cm length and of variable width are sewn together.

5.8 **Knitted Cushion**

This knitted cushion, like the patchwork cushion, offers the possibility to use leather scraps, as you can cut out long leather bands from small leather sections with sharp scissors. (a) Uneven edges and curves are less noticeable if you cut the bands narrowly. The individual leather bands are stitched together inconspicuously at the ends.

The leather cushion shown here measures 50 x 50 cm and was knitted with no. 10 needles, flat right. The leather band width is 5-6 mm, with 34 stitches cast on.

Material and tools
leather scraps
sharp scissors
matching thread, needle
one pair of knitting needles no. 10
wool felt of same color as leather, about 100 gr.
2 buttons or felt buttons

Stitch test

It is important to do a stitch test before knitting. Cast on five stitches and knit five rows. Measure and calculate for 50 cm.

Cushion front side

1. Cast on the calculated number of stitches with both needles so that the stitches lie loosely on the needle. Once enough stitches are cast on, pull out one needle.
2. A pattern stitched flat right is done by knitting right (b, c and d) and purling left. (e, f and g)
3. Once you reach a height of 50 cm, bind off the stitches. Cut off the leather band and pull through the last stitch. (h)

Cushion back side

The back side is made of the same size and color as the front side, only from felt. A wool felt of 65 cm x 80 cm is used as the base. The back side of the cushion is worked the same way as described for the cushion with appliqués.

5.9 **Floor Cushion**

This sit-on cushion is great for relaxing. It radiates calmness and coziness and looks inviting. Although the floor cushion is easy to fabricate, you should allow enough time because of the relatively ample felting involved here. This cushion can be turned with the felt or the leather side up, depending on your choice. Also, both sides can be made from leather.

Material and tools

300 gr. of wool felt (ready-made crossed carding web is best)

soft cow or calf leather, 80 x 80 cm

filling, used here: 3 kg of foam pieces

2 leather buttons

sewing machine

thread

leather needle

extra long needle, about 15 cm

Work stages

1   Cut out a round piece of 1 meter diameter from the carding web. Do the felting as described for the appliqué cushion until you get a circle of 77 cm diameter. Always turn and flip the surface so as to shrink it evenly. Leave to dry.

2   Cut the leather to a circle of 77 cm diameter.

3   Mark the centers of both felt and leather pieces and pin them together top side to top side. Only place pins in the area of the seam allowance. Stitch circumference with a 1 cm seam allowance while leaving an opening of 10 cm for filling.

4   The foam pieces are dense and firm and will not flatten when sitting on them. They also do not require a ticking and can be put directly into the cover. The filling is best done in a bathtub or shower stall due to the absence of static charge. Fill the foam pieces evenly and firmly and close the 10 cm wide opening with a leather needle and thread using the mattress stitch (see page 68). (a)

5   To flatten the cushion, affix a leather button to the center of both the leather and the felt side. Use the long needle with double thread to stitch from the center of the leather side to the center of the felt side (through the cushion) to attach the buttons. You can cover the buttons with scrap leather yourself (see page 60) or have them sewn by someone else. (b)

5.10 **Leather Bottles**

Bottles of all shapes can be covered with leather, just like the bowl in this chapter. Three variations are shown here.

Material and tools	water bowl
leather scraps	sponge
bottle	matching thread
adhesive paper strips	glue
tissue paperr	sewing machine

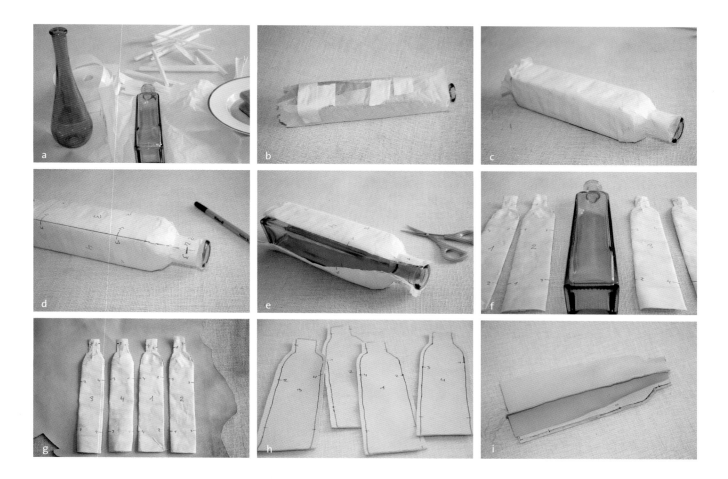

Work stages

1   Firmly wrap the bottle with a thin layer of tissue paper. (a and b)

2   Pull the paper strips with the glue side over the moistened sponge and place them onto the tissue paper so they overlap until the entire bottle has been covered. One overlapping layer is sufficient. Leave the paper strips to dry.

3   Depending on the shape of the bottle, divide the paper cover into three or four sections of similar width, mark them and cut the cover into these same sections. (d and e)

4   Even out the cut lines of these sections. (f)

5   Place the sections on the leather piece and cut with a 0.5 cm seam allowance. (g and h)

6   Glue the seam allowances together back to back and stitch together with a distance of 0.5 cm to the edge. (i)

7   Affix the three or four leather sections to each other, level the top and bottom edge if necessary and cover the bottle.

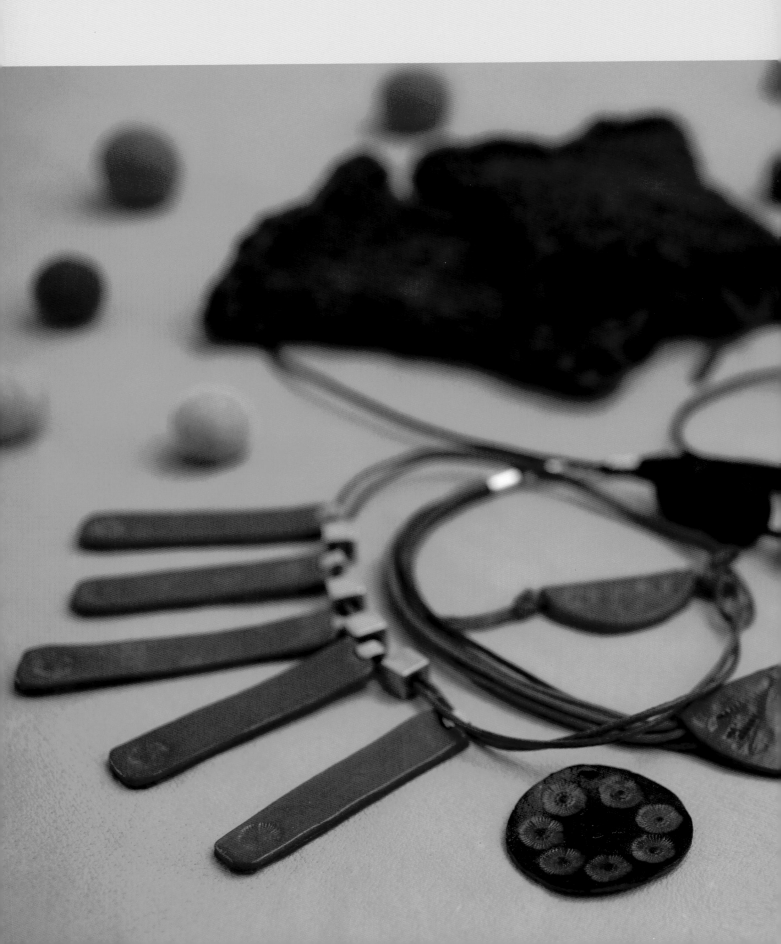

6

Leather Jewelry

6.1 Leather Jewelry Techniques

Since ancient times, leather has inspired humans to adorn themselves. Apart from the desire to warm himself, this necessity for adornment could be the reason why the successful hunter began to wear the skin of the hunted animal. Certainly it was the joy of decorating and adorning himself that led to the dyeing of animal skins.

Artfully tanned leather was already known in Ancient Egypt. Tomb findings have yielded well-preserved red and yellow goat leather, as well as nicely dyed leather bands with embossed flower- and other ornaments. The leather caps which are depicted on wall frescos, with their long extensions covering part of the back, are also made from dyed leather.

There are several Bible passages which speak of dyed leather, for example, the book of Exodus in the Old Testament reports about red dyed ram and goat hides.

For a long time the Japanese and Chinese have had extraordinary knowledge in the areas of leather dyeing, lacquering and artistic design, particularly stamping and embossing.

Document cabinet: body from wood, leather cover, iron fitting, leathercut, embossing and punching © Deutsches Ledermuseum-Schuhmuseum Offenbach

The making of leather containers, sheaths, shoes, and tack by artfully shaping it dates as far back as the Bronze Age. Leather was pulled over a wooden form and sewn together. To increase its strength, several layers were often placed on top of each other. The wooden form could then be removed. However, it was not removed in all cases, as wood and metal objects were covered with this method as well.

Apart from the shaping of leather, it was artistically worked with various decoration techniques mostly developed in the Orient. There are known examples of artistic and ornamental leather workings, like hand gold plating, which initially strongly influenced the earliest European leather decoration and jewelry artisans as to the choice of ornamentations and motifs. Coptic leather objects from the 4th to the 8th century exhibit carving and peeling as well as braiding, embossing, dyeing, and gold plating.

Around the Middle Ages it became common to alter, diminish, or entirely remove the grain of the leather. This leather was used to make sheaths for holy containers and book bindings, and they were either adorned with the ancient technique of blind embossing or by painting them with lacquer or enamel.

One of the earliest influential leather embossing techniques has to be blind embossing, which was generally known around 1300. At first, primarily cow and calf leather was used, from the 16th century on it became mostly pig leather. Only vegetal-tanned leather was used because it was easier to shape and press. Because of the malleability of vegetal-tanned leather, stamps or plates made from boxwood were pressed into the moist leather. This method was also called cold printing, as the wood of the stamp could not be heated. A short time later, metal stamps which could be heated replaced the wooden stamps. These stamps with a diameter of 3 to 4 cm were relatively small, and they were cut so the desired ornament would rise up from the lowered background. There were two main stamp types, the small stamp for ornamentations, where large surfaces were covered with an even pattern, and the large stamp with mainly Christian and heraldic motifs. Blind embossing was not suitable for free and creative leather designs, the only variable was the order of the existing motifs. By adding blind lines the patterns were sectioned or divided. Blind lines were pressed or drawn into the moist leather with a heated iron. This not only resulted in the grooving of the leather, it also darkened it. Efforts to also freely design the reliefs resulted, via modeling, in the leathercut.

Leathercutting was the preferred method for leather ornamentations during the 14th and 15th centuries. An ornamental or figurative drawing was cut into the grain side of the leather and emphasized by driving it from the fleshy side. The important factor for leathercuts was the material, which had to be vegetal-tanned cow or calf leather of at least 1.2 to 1.4 mm. Thinner leather was more likely to cut through it. The leather also had to be elastic, as it was not only cut but modeled as well. The classic leathercut consisted of first laying out an original-sized drawing and pressing it to the leather with a metal pen. The cut was then made with a special three-sided knife, about 0.5 to 0.7 mm deep, while constantly turning the leather. The moistened cut was traced with a hot iron and the edges were fixed. The final step was dyeing the cut.

The leathercut technique was further enhanced while trying to increase the contrast between the background and the motif. The dimensional design was achieved by embossing, a technique which could easily be combined with leathercutting, as both techniques took advantage of the characteristics of moist leather to be shaped, pressed and embossed, or stamped. A punch or stamp was utilized to flatten the leather up to the leathercut edge, so that the motif would stand out from the embossed or stamped background.

Hand gold plating is yet another artistic ornamentation technique. At the end of the 15th century it reached the West from the Orient, first to adorn book covers. Soon it was used to decorate boxes, sheaths, and particularly shields with gold plating. While changing from the leathercutting and blind embossing techniques to gold plating, a change with the material also happened. During the Middle Ages, cow and calf leather was preferred for leathercuts, while the blind embossing a pressing techniques were used later with pig leather. Gold plating was done on the typical oriental dyed goat leather (Moroccan) with its fine grain. Due to the change in decoration, the material changed as well. During the 16th century, cardboard increasingly replaced wood as material for book covers.

The process of hand gold plating involves the pressing of previously heated stamps of gold leaf onto leather according to a previously created design. Since the Middle Ages these stamps consisted of bronze, while those in the Orient were made from hardened leather. One of the problems was the size of the form stamps, which were only the size of a finger nail, while the motifs, often figurative representations, were quite large. The stamps had to be placed in such a way so as to not show any transitions, just like a puzzle. At first, leather was primed with ox blood; later, egg white thinned with vinegar was used. Today, the primer is based on shellac. Once the primer has partly dried, the thin gold leaf is applied onto the warm stamp and pressed onto the leather.

Appliqués can be used to pattern leather items with color. The best method is to draw the desired motif onto a piece of paper, cut it out, and transfer it onto a piece of leather (for example, thin lamb or calf nappa). Cut out the motif with thin scissors and glue it onto the leather to be decorated. Take note that most leather items require a seam allowance, which needs to be free from appliqués. Use a fine stitch (position 2) to stitch the appliqués onto the leather. Minor details can be fixed by using a thin pair of thread or nail scissors.

Adorned edges can be achieved with thin strings or bands of leather, perhaps of contrasting color. Pre-drill the stitches with a punch fork or an awl.

Instead of using a simple machine stitch, edges can be united with a blanket stitch, whip stitch, moccasin, or button hole stitch (see page 67).

Up until a few years ago it was common to adorn leather with various techniques. The natural grain of the leather was completely covered by the rich decorations. Fast-forward to today, where the grain pattern should emphasize

Applications

Gold embossing in Morocco today: a stamp is used to hammer the gold from the foil onto the leather

6.2 **Embossing**

the natural character of leather, as opposed to plastics. Today, the image and the look of natural and used leather dominates leather fashion. When they are greased, waxed, brushed, and sanded, bags and clothing attain a patina and the much-favored used or second-hand look.

When sanding, only use very fine sanding or polishing paper without much pressure and work carefully with circular motions. After greasing or waxing the leather, it attains its patina effect. Before trying out finished items, try out the used look with a piece of leather scrap.

Mechanical graining emphasizes the natural grain pattern. It can be done with both hands, rolling the leather topside to topside over its fold with slight pressure across its entire surface until the grain stands out, or with a ribbed piece of wood (see page 56).

When ironing or rolling leather, the grain pattern disappears. A cloth-like character can be added to the surface by sanding it slightly.

During the times of the Jugendstil or Art Deco, stamped and embossed leather was in such demand that supply could not satisfy demand. For this reason, items from artificial leather such as book covers and writing cases were produced on an industrial scale and embossed with all kinds of patterns.

Material and tools
vegetal-tanned leather
thick linoleum, same as the one used for linoleum cuts, or soft wood apt for woodcuts (i.e. basswood)
tissue paper
carbon paper

Work stages

1. Draw the pattern or motif onto a piece of paper. Larger motifs are more suitable than smaller ones. Turn over the paper and transfer it onto a piece of wood or linoleum with copy or carbon paper.

2. Cut the motifs mirrored, so that the grooves in the plate will appear elevated on the leather.

3. Only vegetal-tanned leather is suitable for embossing and stamping. Soak the leather in warm water, lie it flat and cover it with a damp cloth until the moisture has penetrated the leather completely.

4. Press the motif with the stamp face down onto the grain side of the leather. Leave the leather to dry completely.

5. Add grease to make the leather water resistant again. The embossing is now permanent, only moisture will make the leather soft again and make the motifs disappear. Embossing can be used well with in combination with other decoration techniques.

6.3 **Punching**

The word punching is derived from the italian *punzone*, meaning hole stamp or piercing punch. A punch is a steel rod of about 10 cm length which is used for patterning or ornamentation. The shapes of the punches vary considerably. There are simple spot punches and there are row punches. A punch is used to emboss moist leather with motifs.

Material and tools
vegetal-tanned leather
punch
firm base
punch hammer (wood), rubber hammer or simple metal hammer
bowl with water and a sponge
leather dye or color, leather finish and brush

Work stages

1   Moisten the leather on the fleshy side with a sponge and leave rolled into a damp cloth or rag. If necessary, add moisture.

2   Place the leather onto a firm surface and place the punch on the grain side of the leather so that the motif faces it. Use more or less force while hammering, depending on the desired depth of the motif. Since punches are usually very small (2–15 mm), the decoration is often achieved by lining up several different punches. Keep the leather moistened while working.

3   Once the leather is punched, leave it to dry. Add leather dye or color and conserve with leather finish.

Various punches

6.4 **Cuff Bracelet**

Self-knitted cuff bracelets are nice to wear, not only in winter. With five needles, they can be knitted round, like the leg of a sock.

Material and tools
pig velour or lamb split velour scraps
sharp scissors
5 knitting needles, size 5.0 (in case of nickel allergy, bamboo needles are recommended)

Work stages

1 Cut a 4 mm wide leather band in a spiral along the edge for the leather piece. Wind up the cut leather band.
2 Cast on some 20 stitches. Divide the stitches onto four needles.
3 Knit the first and all following stitches to the right. (a and b)
4 Bind off after 15 cm.

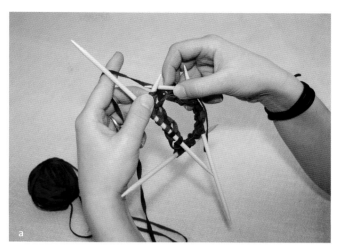

6.5 **Chains** 🜫

Leather chains have one decisive advantage over many other neck chains: they are always very light and warm, and can be worn directly on the skin during summer and winter. Because of their similar properties, leather and felt can be combined with each other very well. Leather chains become more beautiful with time.

Chain I

Material and tools
vegetal-tanned cow leather (scraps)
4 leather strings in distinct red and brown colors
necklace clasp
glue
leather dye and fine brush
different punches
hammer
flat pliers
awl

Work stages

1   Place the cow leather in warm water and leave it rolled up in a damp cloth to allow moisture to be absorbed.

2   Once the leather is well-soaked and soft, which can be checked by the even look on the grain side, cut out two oval pieces. A larger one of 5.5 x 7 cm and a smaller one with diameters of 5 x 3.8 cm. When moist, leather can be cut like butter.

3   Place the leather ovals onto a wooden surface and punch in patterns with the various punches. Leave to dry.

4   Paint the outside of the ovals and leave to dry. (a)

5   Fold the larger leather oval at the center and glue it together, careful not to get any glue into the fold itself, as the leather strings will be pulled though. (b)

6   For the attachment of the smaller leather oval, punch a hole through both layers of the glued large oval. Punch a hole through the smaller oval as well and thread a 4 cm piece of leather string, then knot both ovals together at the back.

7   Double the leather strings and cut to 35 cm. Place glue on the ends and place them into the closure and press with the flat pliers. Thread the pendant over the strings.

You can easily make a ring from a scrap piece of damp leather:

Cut a piece of 2 x 10 cm, punch at your discretion and dye with color after drying. Measure the appropriate finger size plus a section for overlap and punch a hole through both overlapping sections with punch pliers. Place a rivet and set it

Variation: leathercut with stamped lines, lacquered in red and black, with silver lining

Chain II

Material and tools

vegetal-tanned cow leather (scrap piece)

leather string, 1 m long

5 eyelets or loops to suspend the leather pieces

4 4 matching pearls

glue

leather dye and fine brush

punch iron (for the slit)

hammer and flat pliers

Work stages

1 Place the leather briefly into warm water and leave to "sweat" in a damp cloth

2 After about half an hour, cut six leather pieces—five long sections for the pendant and one round piece for the closure—and punch at your discretion.

3 With the punch iron, punch a slit into the upper center of the five leather tongues and leave to dry.

4 Dye the pieces with leather dye or color all around.

5 Press the eyelets or loops into the slits and press them flat with the flat pliers.

6 Double the leather and lay it out, knotting a loop for the closure. The loop should be somewhat smaller than half the size of the round closure piece (see also step 8).

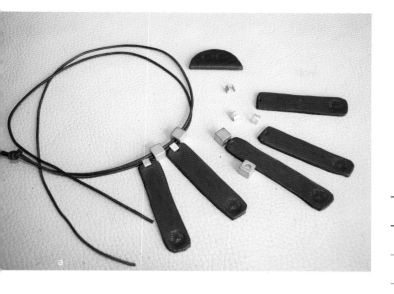

7 Thread the leather tongues and pearls as shown. (a)
8 To make the toggle closure, make a knot some 10 cm from the end of the leather string, fold the round piece of leather around the string and glue it, then add another knot.

Chain III

Material and tools
leather band
leather scraps, for example embossed calf leather
glue
roll cutter
awl
pearl for closure

Work stages

1   Cut the leather scraps into strips of 2 x 12 cm. Two strips of different color make for one roll. (a)

2   Put glue on the fleshy side and carefully roll up the pieces, slightly offset, according to the image. Start out with the inner one and roll up this strip a little, then add the second strip which is supposed to be on the outside. The edges need to line up nicely, and avoid folds and creases. (b)

3   Use the awl to perforate the center and to widen the hole, thread the leather string past the hole. If necessary, use a needle for strings.

4   To make the toggle closure, make a loop at one end of the leather string, thread the pearl and lock with a second knot.

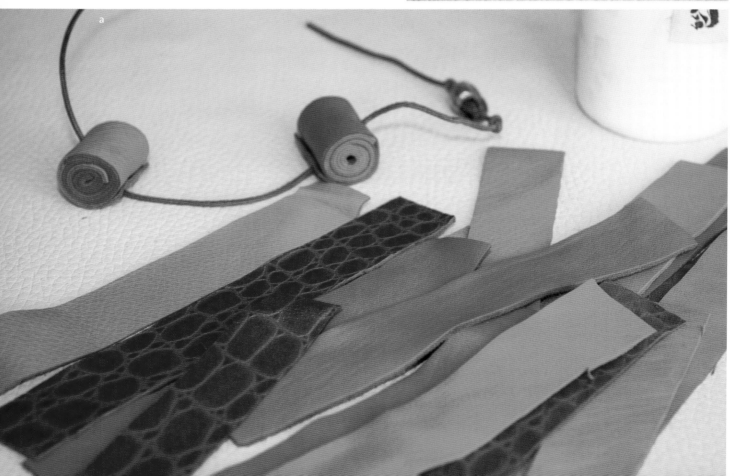

Chain IV

Material and tools

leather band

leather scraps, such as embossed calf leather

glue

roll cutter

awl

steel string or silver wire, 1 m long

about 32 crimp beads

wool fleece, card sliver or scoured wool in different colors

hot soapy water

Work stages

1   Making the felt pearls: roll up a few grams of wool fleece to form a small ball and place inside the hot soapy water. Roll carefully with both hands until you feel that the surface hardens and turns into felt. Now, roll harder until the pearl has the desired firmness and size.

2   As described with Chain III, make the leather pearls.

3   Use the awl to make holes into the felt and leather pearls.

4   Alternate threading the pearls onto the wire or string; before and after each pearl, crimps beads are threaded, and once all pearls are at their correct place, these are pressed tight.

5   When finished, unite both ends of the wire or string with two crimp beads. The chain is long enough to be placed over the head, so a closure is not necessary.

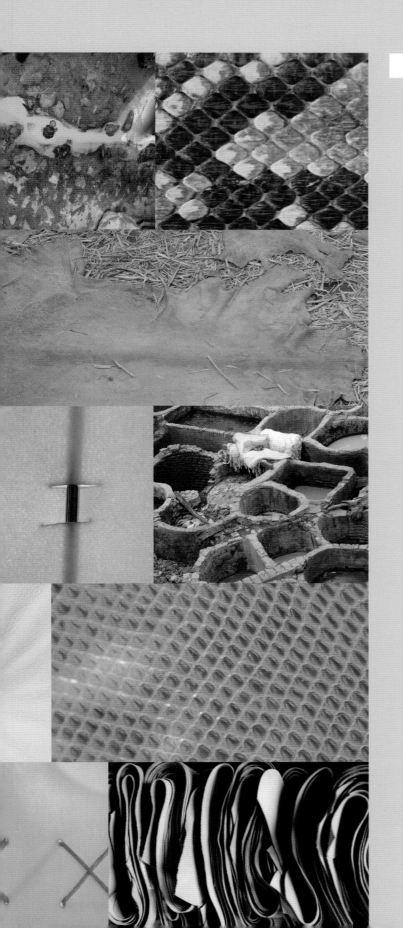

7

Appendix

7.1   Image Credits

The photos on the following pages were made by Josephine Barbe: 12, 18 bottom left, 19, 22 top, 39, 40, 41, 43, 45, 55, 76, 78, 79, 80, 89, 98/99, 103, 105, 106, 107, 112, 113, 115, 116, 118, 128, 131 top, 133 bottom row, 136 left, 143, 145 top, 151, 156, 159 top and center right, 160, 161 162, 163, 164, 165, 166/167

The images on pages 10, 100 and 154 were provided by the German Leather and Shoe Museum Offenbach.

The two images on page 13 are by akg-images.

The images on pages 14 and 16 are from Hamm, *Buch der Erfindungen*.

The images on pages 11, 15 and 28 are taken from Diderot/d'Alembert, *L'Encyclopédie*.

All other photographs by Frank-Michael Arndt.

7.2   Acknowledgments

A very special thanks to my two children Philine and Antonin, who were very considerate with regards to my work.

Much heartfelt thanks goes to Frank-Michael Arndt for the beautiful photos and the inspiring cooperation.

Thanks to the company Fauck and Dago Engler for their valuable insights regarding leather and for authorizing photography sessions in their leather shops.

Thanks to Doris Puschner, Rainer Heinrich and Gabi Seiss for the use of their apartment; the latter has also greatly helped me to compile the photo collage on page 166/167.

I also express my thanks to the team at the Bibliothek des Deutschen Technikmuseums Berlin for kindly providing the archive photos.